Curriculum, Personal Narrative and the Social Future

GW00535768

Recent writing on education and social change, and a growing number of new governmental initiatives across Western societies, have proceeded in denial or ignorance of the personal missions and biographical trajectories of key public sector personnel. This book stems from an underpinning belief that we have to understand the personal biographical if we are to understand the fate of social and political initiatives.

In education, a pattern has emerged in many countries around the world. Each new government enshrines targets and tests to ensure that teachers at the frontline of delivery are 'more accountable'. While this often provides evidence of symbolic action to the electorate or professional audiences, the evidence at the level of service delivery is often far less impressive. Targets, tests and tables may win wide support from the public, but there are often negligible or even contradictory effects at the point of delivery, enforced by the ignorance or denial of personal missions and biographical mandates. This book locates most of its analysis and discussion at the point of culture clash between centralised dictates, and individual and collective life missions. While the early part of the book considers a range of issues related to the school curriculum, the focus on the biographical and life narrative becomes increasingly important as the analysis proceeds.

Curriculum, Personal Narrative and the Social Future will be of key interest to practising teachers, educational researchers and students on teacher training courses, postgraduate courses and doctoral courses.

Ivor F. Goodson is Professor of Learning Theory at the University of Brighton, UK and International Research Professor at the University of Tallinn, Estonia. His most recent books are *Narrative Learning* (2010), *Narrative Pedagogy* (2011) and *Developing Narrative Theory* (2013). For more information please visit: www.ivorgoodson.com..

Curriculum, Personal Narrative and the Social Future

Ivor F. Goodson

Routledge
Taylor & Francis Group

LONDON AND NEW YORK

First published 2014
by Routledge
2 Park Square, Milton Park, Abingdon, Oxon OX14 4RN

and by Routledge
711 Third Avenue, New York, NY 10017

Routledge is an imprint of the Taylor & Francis Group, an informa business

British Library Cataloguing in Publication Data
A catalogue record for this book is available from the British Library

Library of Congress Cataloging in Publication Data
Goodson, Ivor.
Curriculum, personal narrative and the social future / Ivor F. Goodson.
    pages cm
  1. Education and state. 2. Curriculum planning. I. Title.
  LC71.G67 2014
  379–dc23   2013049401

ISBN: 978-0-415-83355-4 (hbk)
ISBN: 978-0-415-83356-1 (pbk)
ISBN: 978-0-203-48934-5 (ebk)

Typeset in Galliard
by Sunrise Setting Ltd, Paignton, UK

Printed and bound in Great Britain by
TJ International Ltd, Padstow, Cornwall

To my dad, Fred, who taught me about love and loyalty.

And to my history teacher at Forest School, Dai Rees,
who opened so many doors.

Contents

Acknowledgements

The following articles have been reproduced with the kind permission of the publishers/editors of the respective journals and books:

'Exploring the teacher's professional knowledge' by I. Goodson and A. Cole, in D. McLaughlin and W.G. Tierney (eds) *Naming Silenced Lives*, pp. 71–94, 1993 (reproduced with permission by Routledge: www.routledge.com).

'The context of cultural inventions: learning and curriculum' by I. Goodson, in P. Cookson and B. Schneider (eds) *Transforming Schools*, pp. 307–27, 1995 (reproduced with permission by Garland Press: http://garlandpress.com).

'The educational researcher as a public intellectual' by I. Goodson, in the *British Educational Research Journal*, 25(3), 1999 (reproduced with permission by www.bera.ac.uk).

'The rise of the life narrative' by I. Goodson, in *Teacher Education Quarterly*, 33(4), 7–21, Fall, 2006 (reproduced with permission by www.teqjournal.org).

'All the lonely people: the struggle for private meaning and public purpose in education' by I. Goodson, in *Critical Studies in Education*, 48(1), March, 131–48, 2007 (reproduced with permission by Taylor and Francis: www.tandf.co.uk).

'Schooling, curriculum, narrative and the social future' by I. Goodson, first appeared in C. Sugrue (ed.) *The Future of Educational Change: International Perspectives*, pp. 123–35, 2008 (reproduced with permission by Routledge: www.routledge.com).

'Curriculum as narration: tales from the children of the colonised' by I. Goodson and R. Deakin Crick, in the *Curriculum Journal*, 2009 (reproduced with permission by Taylor and Francis: www.tandf.co.uk).

'Listening to professional life stories: some cross-professional perspectives' by I. Goodson, in Helle Plauborg and Simon Rolls (eds) *Teachers' Career Trajectories and Work Lives*, pp. 3, 203–10, 2009 (reproduced with permission by Springer: www.springer.com).

'Restructuring teachers' work-lives and knowledge in England and Spain' by I. Goodson, J. Muller, C. Norrie and F. Hernandez, in *Compare: A Journal of Comparative and International Education*, 40(3), 265–77, May, 2010 (reproduced with permission by Taylor and Francis: www.tandf.co.uk).

'Times of educational change: towards an understanding of patterns of historical and cultural refraction' by I. Goodson, in the *Journal of Educational Policy*, 25(6), 767–75, 2010 (reproduced with permission by Routledge: www.routledge.com).

Introduction

In Britain, one of the complaints about the Research Assessment Exercise (now transformed into the REF) is that it causes academics to focus on producing a range of articles rather than books. The result in many cases is that books now often comprise a set of distinctive articles. Whilst this is a correct indictment of the RAE (and successor) I cannot apportion blame in this way for this collection of essays. In my own case, I have always tended to write essays and then collect them into books. Since the essays often echo my scholarly preoccupation at a particular time, I hope they have a coherence and a continuity that moves beyond the disparate and disorderly.

In 2006 I produced a volume of collected works focusing on learning, curriculum and life politics, but the continuity of focus is echoed in this volume, which focuses on the social future. It is perhaps worth once again rehearsing some of my sense of the continuity of purpose, which I believe to be at the heart of the work.

Much of my research is driven by a belief that we have to understand the personal and biographical if we are to understand the social and political. This far from unique insight nonetheless allows us to scrutinise the educational enterprise from a highly productive vantage point. So much of recent writing on educational and social change (and likewise so many new governmental initiatives) across Western societies has proceeded in denial or ignorance of the personal missions and biographical trajectories of key personnel. This is nowhere more true than in contemporary Britain, where the government's disregard and palpable ignorance of personal missions is becoming legendary. Whilst this often provides evidence of 'symbolic action' to electorates or professional audiences the evidence at the level of service delivery is often far less impressive. Sometimes the symbolic enshrinement of targets, tests and tables, whilst winning wide constituency support at the outset, proves later to have had often negligible or even contradictory effects at the point of delivery. The point of contradiction is often the ignorance or denial of personal missions and biographical mandates. These therefore seem a good place to locate our studies (and indeed our policies), not reluctantly at the end of a process, but enthusiastically at the beginning.

In a range of books I have examined the social political process by which school subjects become 'timeless givens' in the grammar of schooling. In fact the 'traditional subjects' turn out to be examples of the 'invention of tradition' as is so much else in our social world. Traditions that endure in the arena of schooling and curriculum must appeal to powerful 'constituencies' and, without that support, new challenges can never gain traction. The tradition of school subjects, therefore, is broadly harmonised with the external constituencies of power. Curriculum approaches that might seek to educate more disadvantaged groups must 'run the gauntlet' of the powerful external constituencies. In the current governmental regime this begins to resemble the 'Charge of the Light Brigade with a fusillade from the Eton rifles added in'. Sustainability in the world of the school curriculum is therefore closely equated with the resonance achieved with external constituencies.

In my first book *School, Subject and Curriculum Change* (Goodson 1983) I noted the distinction between domination and structure, and mechanism and mediation. This means that any assertion about curriculum must be located within the historical period in question. At certain points, new structures are established that set up new 'rules of the game'. Whilst this establishment of new structures might be viewed as domination, the period that follows such legislation is one of mediation. The period of the 1960s and early 1970s was one of social innovation in much of the Western world. In this period, there were social missions and social movements aiming at social justice and social inclusion. These missions and movements led to serious pedagogic and schooling experiments to broaden social inclusion. My point in covering some of these alternative pedagogies was not to argue that these provided an answer to the perennially elusive project of social inclusions, but to delineate the purposes, pedagogies and practices that were developed as part of this social movement. In later periods 'social inclusion' again surfaced, but this time as an uncoupled political rhetoric located within a far more stratifying strategy of educational provision. Since this rhetoric showed little interest in the earlier experiments and social movements, it was difficult to believe in its serious purpose. Schools are weighted with contextual inertia and to completely ignore history in this way is to be either naïve or duplicitous; it is certainly not to be properly informed or educationally purposeful.

But this is to run ahead, for by the millennium much had changed and the reversals of the period following Margaret Thatcher's election in 1979 and Ronald Reagan's in 1980 have been well documented. For instance, in England, the similarity between the 1904 structure of secondary education and the 1988 National Curriculum is pointed up. I note that the 1904 structure embodied that curriculum offered to the grammar school clientele as opposed to the curriculum being developed in the Board Schools and aimed primarily at the working class. At this point, dominant interest groups were acting to favour one segment or vision over another. In the years following the Second World War and culminating in the 1960s, more egalitarian forces brought the creation of comprehensive schools, where children of all classes came under one roof. Some curriculum initiatives sought to redefine and challenge the hegemony of the grammar school curriculum and associated pattern of social prioritising. It was to defeat this challenge that some of the policies of the Thatcher government were formulated, notably the National Curriculum. Seeking in turn to challenge and redirect these reforms and intentions, the political right has argued for the rehabilitation of the 'traditional' (i.e. grammar school) subjects. The National Curriculum can be seen as a political statement of the victory of the forces and intentions representing these political groups. A particular vision, a preferred segment of the nation, has therefore been reinstated and prioritised, as legislated and as 'national'.

The changing configuration of curriculum provides us with a valuable litmus test of social and political intentions and purposes. As we can see, these configurations change as the balance of social forces and the underlying economic landscape undergo cyclical change; this can be witnessed in many Western countries during a similar pattern of experimentation in pursuit of social justice in the late 1960s and early 1970s. All schools were affected by the progressive desire to build a 'Great Society', characterised by social inclusion and social justice. Whilst some schools pursued 'root and branch' revolutionary change (as with the comprehensive schools mentioned in Chapter 2), others pursued social inclusion within a more conventional grammar of schooling.

The pattern of reversal noted was similarly evident with the introduction of standards-based testing and new patterns of systems differentiation (e.g. Magnet Schools). This was part of a world movement to transform schooling, often in ways that resonated with the emerging new economic world order. Some commentators have called this 'market fundamentalism', bringing in a competitive business ethos around notions of school effectiveness and school choice. This progressive marketisation of schooling had many implications: one was to sideline the significance of the struggle over different kinds of curriculum. Differentiation of life chances through curriculum was progressively passed over to the work of the market in disbursing resources according to particular school sites and systems, related increasingly closely to patterns of residential location.

The seismic social and political changes at the end of the twentieth century, which are echoed in the educational transformations noted above, pose a challenge for those concerned with investigating them. The changing positionality of curriculum as a distributor of life chances and the salience of tests, targets and tables has moved the focus of social and political action. Our studies therefore need to reflect this transformation and reconceptualise both the substantive focus of inquiry and the methods employed.

From the beginning, I have argued that we have to understand the personal and biographical if we are to understand the social and political. This is nowhere more true than in the relevance of personal biography in the choice of research focus and method. I have tried to show 'where I am coming from' and this illuminates a clear predisposition in favour of strategies for social inclusion and social justice. But I have also tried to provide a historical context for understanding social possibilities. Hobsbawm's golden age of egalitarianism, which culminated in the 1960s and 1970s, has clearly passed, and some personal nostalgia is patently evident in some of my accounting (Hobsbawm 1994). But I do seek to avoid and warn against golden age reminiscences for, as Lasch has reminded us, nostalgia is the abdication of memory (Lasch 1979). I should therefore note a few of the myths of the golden age. Many public services, schools included, developed a culture that favoured service providers rather than clients and customers and, at times, trade union action sometimes exacerbated the problem. Public and professional groups can hijack resources for their own purposes, just as other groups can. And progressive practices can develop areas of looseness, non-accountability and professional self-aggrandisement if so permitted. In many ways, Britain in the 1970s provided a case study of such behaviour, ending as it did in a 'winter of discontent' amongst workers and trade unions, which ushered in the Thatcher government.

The exhumation of the conflicts of the 1970s, the attribution of blame and delineation of causes is an ongoing task for historians. Their importance for the arguments in this book is to point out that all was not as it should be in the public services before the more recent reforms and restructuring. Whilst the best professionals adopted a 'caring vocationalism' in providing social inclusion, many examples of self-serving professionalism could be found. The task, as always, was to try to understand both the larger social movements of reform but also their specific embodiment and embeddedness within personal biographies.

This book has sought to employ this focus from the beginning and in the later chapters will make both the methodological and substantive argument for an increasing focus on 'life politics': I believe the new world order makes this even more important than it was in the earlier periods examined above. This is partly because of the triumph of 'the individualised society' – more than ever, in this context, individual life politics becomes the site of social contestation. Once the focus was on collective social movements, say for school or curriculum change. Now a primary strategy for understanding social change should focus on the individuals' life politics.

In Part I, I begin to review the relationship between work – or the social construction of curriculum-emerging work – on historical periodisation, and some tentative visions of curriculum and narration.

In Chapter 1 curriculum change processes are reviewed, together with the transformations in curriculum control that developed in recent decades. In Britain a pattern of increasing corporate takeover can be discerned in patterns of curriculum definition. This has led to a systematic denial of expertise as constituted by the existing educational community (referred to as 'the blob', by the current Minister for Education). In general, denial of expertise is not a smart move when viewed from an educational point of view or from the view of the children being educated. When viewed through the economic viewpoint, seeing education as a site of 'profit' and accumulation, it may of course look very different. In some government circles, this is all too obviously the viewpoint that is being privileged.

In Chapter 2, I review my work on curriculum change and curriculum construction in the light of a growing sense of historical periodisation. In Chapters 3 and 4, the current crisis of curriculum change is conceptualised and delineated in ways that lead towards a re-conceptualisation of the working curriculum.

In Chapter 3, I have sought to bring together the work on historical periods and curriculum re-conceptualisation to develop our understanding of how curriculum is re-contextualised and how it deals with the modalities of cultural and historical refraction. This work grows out of the recent seven-member-state European project PROFKNOW, which looked at professional knowledge and its delineation in seven countries of the European Union. The theory of refraction seeks to understand how curriculum is invented and instantiated in different ways in different social settings. The work provides a link to Part II, in that the role of human agency, personal narratives and missions, and specific cultural milieu, is placed at the centre of the analysis.

In Part II, the move towards a greater consideration of professional life missions, professional knowledge and professional narratives is developed. In Chapter 5, I look at the emergence of forms of life narrative as a cultural phenomenon of post-modernity and neo-liberalism. The focus on individual and personal missions is explored as a cultural creation of a particular historical period. This of course links with the arguments in Part I, about the specificity of historical periods and how these contingencies affect people's sense of personal mission, personal identity and political and professional affiliation.

Chapters 6 and 7 focus on how people's life missions and identity projects impinge on their professional life and work. Studying this juxtaposition is a crucial lens for interrogating the way in which restructuring initiatives work with or collide with people's identity projects and life missions.

In Part III, in Chapters 8 and 9, these perspectives are reviewed in a wider collective and political milieu. The concern here is to explore the capacity of qualitative methods like life history to generate new public discourses and public intellectual modalities. In Chapter 10 the focus on knowledge and personal narrative is brought together and examined for its capacity to inform our social future.

References

Goodson, I.F. (1983) *School Subjects and Curriculum Change*, London, Sydney and Dover: Croom Helm.

Hobsbawm, E. (1994) *The Age of Extremes*, New York: Vintage.

Lasch, C. (1979) *The Culture of Narcissism: American Life in an Age of Diminishing Expectations*, New York: W.W. Norton & Co, Inc.

PROFKNOW (2002–8) PROFKNOW Professional Knowledge in Education and Health (PROFKNOW) (2002–8) 'Restructuring work and life between state and citizens in Europe', Brighton, UK: University of Brighton, Sweden: University of Gothenburg, Athens: National and Kopodistorian University of Athens, Finland: University of Joensuu, Spain: University of Barcelona, Portugal: University of the Azores, Ireland: St. Patrick's College, Dublin City University, Sweden: University of Stockholm. Available at: http://www.ips.gu.se/english/Research/research_programmes/pop/current_research/PROFKNOW/ (accessed 6 September 2013).

Part I

1 Curriculum change processes and historical periods

In historical terms, it is not at all surprising that 'change forces' and pervasive restructuring initiatives should be sweeping the world at the moment. Since 1989, we have seen a seismic shift in the world in terms of the dominant political ideologies. Beyond the triumphalist 'end of history' line peddled by camp followers lies the belief that American democratic and business values have now vanquished all alternative political and economic systems. Behind this ideological shift is, of course, a massive technological transformation, which many believe puts us within a 'third industrial revolution'. Such huge transformations, quite understandably, lead to a passing belief that history is now irrelevant, suspended, over.

But in the everyday world of social life and social institutions, this glib dismissal of history does not stand scrutiny for a moment. Can the situation in Gaza, Syria or Iraq really transcend history? In the end, won't the change forces, with all their smart bombs and surveillance technology, nonetheless have to confront human and historical fabric? The answer, of course, is inevitably that transformational change forces will have to confront and engage with existing patterns of life and understanding.

In terms of educational changes, John Meyer *et al.* (1992) talked about school reforms as 'world movements' that sweep across the global arena: invented in one country, they are rapidly taken up by political elites and powerful interest groups in each country. But what then becomes clear is that these world movements of school reform 'embed' themselves in national school systems in very different ways. The national school systems are *refractors* of world change forces (see Goodson 2010). Our task is to understand this process of social refraction, for only then can we develop a change theory that is sensitive to the circumstances, albeit deeply changed circumstances, of schooling.

In his book, *Fluctuating Fortunes*, Vogel (1988) documented the changing cycles of power of global business. In periods of high business power, schooling tends to be driven towards business values. These periods move educational policy and economic policy into close harmony. At such times, educational questions tend to be driven hard by vocational questions; issues of competitiveness and economic efficiency are widely promoted. But the educational and the economic are, as a matter of fact, not synonymous. Sometimes they can be performed in harmony, but at other times they lead in very different directions if the educational needs of school students are scrutinised in their own right. At times, when business power is held in balance by other forces, the 'internal' professional power of educator groups can emerge as a major defining force.

Such a period began in the years after the Second World War. This period of 'cold war' between political ideologies set capitalist business values against systems of Communist production. In the West, egalitarian social policies were pursued and public education systems were heavily promoted as vehicles of common purpose and social good. Business values and the private sector lived in 'mixed economies', where public sectors provided a good deal of the 'public services' of national systems.

In this period, which lasted well into the 1970s – even into the 1990s in some countries (for example, Canada) and into the present in other countries (for example, Finland) – educators were seen as having large amounts of professional autonomy. Much educational change was, at this time, left to internal educational experts, to initiate and define.

In these historical circumstances of substantial professional autonomy, change theory looked for the sources of initiation and promotion of change to the educator groups 'internal to the school systems'. In conceptualising curriculum change in the 1970s, I developed a model that scrutinised the 'internal affairs' of change and set this against the 'external relations' of change.

Internal educational change

One example of the internal patterns of change that predominated in the 1960s and 1970s were the models of curriculum change that were developed in a range of work I conducted at that time. For instance, the model of school subject change, which provided a four-stage evolutionary pattern, was defined in Goodson (1995) in the following way:

1 *Invention* may come about from the activities or ideas of educators; sometimes as a response to 'climates of opinion' or pupil demands or resistance or from inventions in the 'outside world': 'The ideas necessary for creation... are usually available over a relatively prolonged period of time in several places. Only a few of these inventions will lead to further action' (Ben-David and Collins 1966).

2 *Promotion* by educator groups internal to the educational system. Inventions will be taken up 'where and when persons become interested in the new idea, not only as intellectual content but also as a means of establishing a new intellectual identity and particularly a new occupational role'. Hence, subjects with low status, poor career patterns and even with actual survival problems may readily embrace and promote new inventions such as environmental studies. Conversely, high-status subjects may ignore quite major opportunities as they are already satisfactorily resourced and provide existing desirable careers. The response of science groups to 'technology' or (possibly) contemporary mathematics groups to

'computer studies' are cases in point. Promotion of invention arises from a perception of the possibility of basic improvements in occupational role and status.

3 *Legislation*. The promotion of new inventions, if successful, leads to the establishment of new categories or subjects. Whilst promotion is initially primarily internally generated, it has to develop external relations with sustaining 'constituencies'. This will be a major stage in ensuring that new categories or subjects are fully accepted, established and institutionalised. And further, that having been established, they can be sustained and supported over time. Legislation is associated with the development and maintenance of those discourses or legitimating rhetorics which provide automatic support for correctly labelled activity.

4 *Mythologization*. Once automatic support has been achieved for a subject or category, a fairly wide range of activities can be undertaken. The limits are any activities which threaten the legitimated rhetoric and hence constituency support. The subject at this point is mythological. It represents essentially a licence that has been granted (or perhaps a 'patent' or 'monopoly rights'), with the full force of the law and establishment behind it. At this point when the subject has been successfully 'invented', the process of invention and of establishment is completed.

(Goodson 1995: 193–4)

It is possible to restate this model of school subject change as a more general educational change model. Hence:

1 invention might be seen as change formulation;
2 promotion as change implementation;
3 legislation as policy establishment;
4 mythologisation as established or permanent change.

But the most important conclusion that can be drawn from studying these patterns of change in the 1960s and 1970s is to evidence how internally generated change works its way towards external legitimation. Of course, it is true that such internally generated change exists in externally contrived climates of opinion, but the important point is that the invention and generation of the change idea begins internally and then works for external legitimation. As we have seen, during the period following the Second World War, and well into the 1970s and 1980s, public service provision was left largely in the hands of professional groups. In this sense, education was left in the hands of teachers and educationalists; it was deemed to be their responsibility to initiate and promote educational change. Whilst occasionally these changes were responses to external stimuli, by and large, the development of external opinion came in the later stages of change establishment. Educational change was, therefore, defined, instigated and promoted internally, and then went on to sustain and win external support in order to ensure establishment and legislation.

External relations of change

Until the late 1970s, internally generated change remained the lynchpin of the change theory that was subsequently codified and written. Since the triumph of Western corporatism in 1989, it is important to revisit the assumption that change is internally generated according to explicitly educational criteria and analyse the kinds of patterns of educational change that now prevail.

I have argued that internal change agents faced a 'crisis of positionality' (Goodson 1999). This crisis of positionality prevails where the balance of change forces is substantially *inverted*. Now change can be seen as invented and originating within external constituencies. In this situation, internal change agents find themselves responding to, not initiating, changes. Thus, instead of being progressive change agents, they often take up the role of conservative respondents (sometimes conservative in the sense of wanting to conserve existing practices) to the externally initiated change. Since educational change is not in line with their own defined missions, it is often seen as alien, unwelcome and hostile. The crisis of positionality for internal change agents is, then, that the progressive internal change agent can become the conservative, resistant and reluctant change agent of external wishes.

For these reasons, above all, change theory has to now develop a finer sense of history. Where change was the internal mission of educators and external relations were developed later, educational goodwill and a sense of purpose and passion might be assumed. Now the educator groups are less initiating agents or partners, and more deliverers of externally defined purposes. Educators have often moved from being proactive and constructive, to becoming reactive and compliant.

To examine these emerging patterns, in the period 1998–2001, Andy Hargreaves and I worked on a new multi-site project examining change in American and Canadian schools. Our primary concern was to analyse and historically compare the changing 'conditions of change'. Our methodology was, as a result, both historical and ethnographic (Goodson 1995).

In the schools we have studied, we have developed a historical archive of the changes and reforms that have been attempted within them. Over time, we have begun to see how educational change follows a series of cycles, not unlike that of the economy. Indeed, we begin to see how, just as Kondratiev (1984) argued, economic change often occurs in long-wave as well as short-wave cycles – so too does educational change.

In these cycles, the powers of internal professional groups and external constituencies oscillate quite markedly and, in doing so, affect the change forces and associated change theories that we analyse and define.

Let me provide an example: the Durant School, in an industrial city in upper New York State, was initiated and promoted by internal educator groups in the late 1960s. One group was concerned to establish an urban learning environment of a broadly progressive character and began to build up a new educational infrastructure in the city centre. A student clientele was attracted as the educators defined and promoted their educational mission. In due course, a loose coalition of like-minded schools grew up and ideas and materials were exchanged. The change forces, then, had some of the features of a social movement. In the later stages, the school began to negotiate with external constituencies – parents, local business, school boards – and, in due course, became a member, albeit a radical one, of the local school system.

More recently, though, patterns of change have begun to change radically towards the pattern of inversion noted earlier. Now, the school primarily responds to change developed by external groups.

For instance, in the sponsorship of new buildings and resources, the role of local business, e.g. Citibank, has been central. There, the consent and collaboration of local business interests have begun to influence school policy. Moreover, local business groups have been hugely influential in pushing for new educational 'standards' and in initiating and promoting major educational changes. 'Schools without walls' has followed progressive practice in stressing course work and project work as a way of assessing student achievement. The school is now challenged by the new mandate, pushed by the school board commissioners, to have students sit the Regents' Examination. This will transform the context and control of the school's curriculum and, in doing so, change the teaching/learning milieu. In the new change dispensation, change is externally mandated and only then internally negotiated.

In contemporary conditions of change, combining ethnographic and historical methods of inquiry provides us with the database to develop a new contextually sensitive change theory. This new theory allows us to arbitrate between the changing balance of external relations and internal affairs in contemporary historical circumstances. I have defined a reformulated change model, which is based on the evidence gathered in these research projects (Goodson 2001) around the millennial years:

1 *Change formulation*: educational changes are discussed in a variety of external arenas including business groups, associated think-tanks, new pressure groups like 'standards mean business' and a variety of relatively newly formed parental groups. Often these changes resemble world movements that can be traced back to the World Bank and the International Monetary Fund (Torres 2000). Much of the change is driven by a belief in the marketisation of education and the delivery of educational services to parental 'consumers', who are free to choose and to bargain over their provision (Kenway 1993; Whitty 1997; Robertson 1998).

2 *Change promotion*: this is handled in a similar fashion by external groups, with varied internal involvement. As Reid (1984) has written:

external forces and structures emerge, not merely as sources of ideas, promptings, inducements and constraints, but as definers and carriers of the categories of content, role and activity to which the practice of schools must approximate in order to attract support and legitimization.

(Reid 1984: 68)

3   *Change legislation*: which provides the legal inducement for schools to follow externally mandated changes. In some countries, schools are evaluated by examination results (which are published in league tables). Measures also exist, or are underway, to link teachers' pay to teachers' performance in terms of students' examination or test results (Menter *et al.* 1997). Such legislation leads to a new regime of schooling, but allows teachers to make some of their own responses in terms of pedagogy and professionalism. Overall, school change policies, and curricula and assessment policies, are thereby legislated, but some areas of professional autonomy and associated arenas for change can still be carved out. In certain countries (for example, Scandinavia), this is leading to progressive decentralisation and a push for new professional autonomy. Again, the world movements for change are historically refracted by national systems.

4   *Change establishment*: whilst external change has been established systematically and legally, the power resides mostly in the new *categorical* understandings of how schools operate – delivering a mandated curriculum, being assessed and inspected, responding to choice and consumer demands (Hargreaves *et al.* 2001). Much of the marketisation of schools is taken for granted now in many countries and, in that sense, has achieved mythological status (ibid.: 51–2).

The period since 2000 has been a period of tumultuous change and instability in financial and economic systems. It has, however, been a period where, in spite of the financial crisis which began in 2007, the forces of corporatisation have consolidated their hold on the social infrastructure. As Michael Sandel notes, we have begun to globally move from being a market economy to becoming a market society – everything is now saleable and available as a site for profit-making (Sandel 2012). This leads to a pervasive sense of 'inversion' at many levels. So, for instance, we now see the 'inversion of democracy' – a system that was once set up to represent the people against vested power now seems to represent vested power (especially corporate power) against the people. As Mirowski shows in his wonderful study, 'neoliberalism has become a "theory of everything" providing a pervasive account of self and identity, knowledge and information, economy and government' (Mirowski 2013).

To state this in terms of society and governance: we would seem to be entering a period of 'corporate rule', where all criteria fit the prevailing neo-liberal dogma and where, as David Graeber (Graeber 2013) has shown, even alternative imaginary possibilities are clinically and forcefully expunged. I have long argued that the curriculum provides a prism, a litmus test, through which to see and test societal health and character. So how the curriculum functions under corporate rule becomes a contemporary question of preeminent importance.

Central to the new world of curriculum is the denial of existing expertise. Education researchers and education professors are summarily consigned to the dustbin of history. In England, their work is seldom considered in government circles and the Minister for Education has publicly derided educational experts with wide experience of educational practices and curriculum design. Any criticism is met with name-calling, e.g. 'the enemies of promise' or 'yadda yadda'. The implication is that the educational expert is a talking head without educational experience. This is classic case of inversion for, of course, it is the government minister who is the talking head without educational experience.

Any detailed analyses of the educational sources for governmental decisions show how superficial policy framing has become – it is based on a mix of selective evidence, intuitive prejudice and corporate influence. In responding to critics of the National Curriculum for History, Michael Gove listed 12 distinguished historians who, he claimed, supported his views. Three of them lived outside Britain, in the United States. Only three have ever taught history at British universities and two were associated with Conservative think-tanks. One of the historians referred to was a sitting Tory MP.

In early 2013, Gove complained that 'survey after survey has revealed disturbing historical ignorance' amongst school children. A retired teacher obtained details of the surveys Gove was referring to by a Freedom of Information Request to which the Department of Education had to respond. It became clear that the evidence-base was selective, partial and paltry. The teacher referred to a poll conducted by a Tory insider, Lord Ashcroft. As Richard Evans, Professor of History at Cambridge University, notes: 'The rest, including a poll carried out by the hotel chain Premier Inn, was either amateurish, politically biased or irrelevant' (Evans 2013: 29). Downes noted that:

> Premier Inn's survey was a marketing exercise taken at face value by gullible journalists. The Politica study (a right-wing think-tank) wasn't a survey and the final two were articles about surveys. An internal search found no details of either.
>
> (ibid. 29)

On such an evidence base, government decisions or curriculum appear to be made. Very clearly the denial of expertise is a strongly held conviction in government decision-making processes.

But why is it so important that educational expertise must be purged? The experience of the Aurora Academies Trust is suggestive of an answer. This was an academy running four schools and paying its American parent company £100,000 a year to use its patented global curriculum. Aurora pays Mosaica, an American subsidiary company, £100 per pupil per year in royalties to use its curriculum. There are 1,000 children in the four schools, which means a yearly profit of £100,000. As Christine Blower, General Secretary of the National Union of Teachers, noted:

> This is taxpayers' money which should be targeted directly at children's education in the classroom. What is most shocking is that no accountability mechanism exists to prevent this, nor is there any form of quality assurance.
>
> (Doward, *The Observer*, 19 May 2013: 11)

In fact, Ofsted (the inspection agency) itself criticised this curriculum for lacking any 'local focus'.

Interestingly, the links between the UK government and Aurora are close: 'It has "lead sponsor" status with the Department of Education, meaning it is consulted on policy decisions and is likely to run more schools in the future' (ibid. 11).

The reasons for the denial of educational expertise then begin to clarify. The handover of curriculum control, and abdication of the use of educational criteria, opens the way for corporate entry into the curriculum field.

Let us review how the curriculum works in the period of corporate rule:

1   *Statement of desired objectives*: defined by internal groups located in think-tanks, world bodies and corporate groups. Stressing economic competitiveness and issues of economy and neo-liberal restructuring. Education has little stated value for itself, only for 'getting a job' or helping the economy.
2   *Translation of economic objectives into 'educational cover story'*: instrumentalisation of value systems and promotion of market objectives within the educational domain. Education and curriculum have become similar to any other commodity.
3   *Delineation of 'rules of operation' for education*: commercialisation of school procedures and practices, and stratification through differentiation. Stress of competitive exams and the organisation of league tables. Teachers are viewed as technicians, who implement this system and are paid by results.
4   *Mandates and manipulation*: mandatory legislation of economic objectives is expressed as educational mechanisms. 'Moral panics' are encouraged in the corporate-owned media about public education – the progressive commercialisation of educational sectors, fees charged 'for profit schools', etc. Corporate penetration of schools and the commercialisation of the curriculum (e.g. defining a common core in many of the states of the USA and their provision in textbooks published by the corporate giant agencies).

Conclusions and complexities

The moving matrix of change models and theories has taken us from a confident belief in professionally generated internal change to triumphantly proclaimed and externally mandated change. The move is now well enough established for us to begin to interrogate externally mandated change for its capacity to sustain new reforms. The acid test is *the sustainability of change*.

The key lacuna in externally mandated change is the link to teachers' professional beliefs and to teachers' own personal missions. In the previous model of change, this was built in as an integral part of the model; in the externally mandated model, it is merely 'assumed'.

All the evidence that is now gathering shows this assumption to be patently false. The personal and professional commitment that must exist at the heart of any new changes and reforms is absent. Not only is it neutrally absent, it is in fact positively absent in the sense that there is a mixture of profound indifference and active hostility to so many changes and reforms.

Profound indifference is apparent, in the sense that many teachers report a moving of their centre of gravity towards personal and social missions 'outside' their professional life. Active hostility is also evident, and arises because so many changes seem ill-conceived, professionally naïve and against the heart and spirit of professional belief.

This, however, seems to have little influence on the reformers. Quite plainly the driving force for these changes is not educational at all. The impetus is a corporative drive to colonise public education as a site for profit accumulation. The ongoing denial and denigration of educational expertise and opinions merely confirms this point.

References

Ben-David, T. and Collins, R. (1966) 'Social factors in the origins of a new science: the case of psychology', *American Sociological Review*, 31, 4.

Doward, J. (2013) 'Academy pays £100,000 for U.S. curriculum', *The Observer*, 19 May.

Evans, R. (2013) 'The Mr Men game', *The New Statesman*, 17–23 May, 29.

Goodson, I.F. (1995) *The Making of Curriculum: Collected Essays*, 2nd edition, London, New York and Philadelphia: Falmer Press.

Goodson, I.F. (1999) 'The educational researcher as a public intellectual', *British Educational Research Journal*, 25, 3.

Goodson, I.F. (2001) 'Social histories of educational change', *Journal of Educational Change*, 2(1), 45–63.

Goodson, I.F. (2003) *Professional Knowledge, Professional Lives: Studies in Education and Change*, Maidenhead and Philadelphia: Open University Press.

Goodson, I.F. and Lindblad, S. (eds) (2010) *Professional Knowledge and Educational Restructuring in Europe*, Rotterdam, Boston and Taipei: Sense.

Graeber, D. (2013) *The Democracy Project: A History, a Crisis, a Movement*, London: Allen Lane.

Hargreaves, A., Earl, L., Moore, S. and Manning, S. (2001) *Learning to Change: Teaching beyond Subjects and Standards*, San Francisco: Jossey-Bass.

Kenway, J. (1993) *Economizing Education: The Post-Fordist Directions*, Geelong, Victoria: Deakin University Press.

Kondratiev, N.D. (1984) *The Long Wave Cycle* (translated by Guy Daniels), New York: Richardson & Snyder.

Menter, I., Muschamp, Y., Nicholls, P., Ozga, J. and Pollard, A. (1997) *Work and Identity in the Primary School: a Post-Fordist Analysis*, Buckingham: Open University Press.

Meyer, J.W., Kamens, D.H. and Benavot, A. (1992) *School Knowledge for the Masses*, London and Washington, DC: Falmer Press.

Mirowski, P. (2013) *Never Let a Serious Crisis go to Waste: How Neoliberalism Survived the Financial Meltdown*, London and New York: Versus.

Reid, W.A. (1984) 'Curricular Topics as Institutional Categories: Implications for Theory and Research in the History and Sociology of School Subjects', in I.F. Goodson and S.J. Ball (eds) *Defining the Curriculum: Histories and Ethnographies*, pp. 67–75, London and Philadelphia: Falmer Press.

Robertson, H.-J. (1998) *No More Teachers, No More Books: The Commercialization of Canada's Schools*, Toronto, Ontario: McClelland & Stewart Inc.

Sandel, M. (2012) *What Money Can't Buy: The Moral Limits of Markets*, London and New York: Allen Lane.

Torres, R.M. (2000) *One Decade of Education for All: The Challenge Ahead [Una Decada de Educacion para Todos: la tasrea pendiente]*, FUM-TEP, Montevideo: Editorial Popular, Madrid: Editorial Laboratorio Educativo, Caracas: IIPE UNESCO, Buenos Aires: Artmed Editoria, Porto Alegre.

Vogel, D. (1988) *Fluctuating Fortunes: The Political Power of Business in America*, New York: Basic Books.

Whitty, G. (1997) 'Marketization, the State, and the Re-formation of the Teaching Profession', in A.H. Halsey, H. Lauder, P. Brown and A.S. Wells (eds) *Education: Culture, Economy, Society*, New York: Oxford University Press.

2 The context of cultural inventions
Learning and curriculum

Schooling, certainly in the particular form it takes in state systems, is a relatively recent invention. The emergence of national systems of schooling has been the subject of a number of recent studies (Ramirez and Boli 1987: 2–17). In this work, as we shall see later, a number of common features can be discerned, as mass schooling systems were developed in the nation states of Western Europe (Boli 1989).

The social and political construction of mass schooling derived much from previous constructions at work in higher and religious education. For instance, from Mir's analysis of the origins of the construction of 'classes' as organisational units, we learn that they were first described in the statutes of the College of Montaigne in France:

> It is in the 1509 programme of Montaigne that one finds for the first time in Paris, a precise and clear division of students into classes.... That is, divisions graduated by stages or levels of increasing complexity according to the age and knowledge required by students.
>
> (Quoted in Hamilton and Gibbons 1980: 7)

Mir argues that the College of Montaigne in fact inaugurated the Renaissance class system in education – but the vital connection to reconstruct is how organisation in classes came to be associated with a curriculum prescribed and sequenced for stages or levels.

The Jesuits were one of the first religious groups to establish a tradition of highly centralised curriculum control within schools. The *Ratio Studiorum* was 'arguably the most systematic course of study ever devised. This carefully graded curriculum organised into classes foreshadowed the "standards" or grades that later became a basic organizing principle for all western systems of education' (Tomkins 1986: 13). The Jesuits carried their systems to many countries. In Canada, for instance, the Jesuit College in Quebec was founded in 1635 (a year before Harvard College was founded in Massachusetts). The curriculum (French was the language of instruction) comprised Latin, Greek, the teaching of grammar, rhetoric and philosophy, as well as history, geography and mathematics.

In terms of Anglo-Saxon origins, the Oxford English Dictionary locates the earliest source of the word 'curriculum' as 1633 in Glasgow. Hamilton believes that Glasgow was a focal area because of the influence of the religious ideas of Calvin (1509–64):

> As Calvin's followers gained political as well as theological ascendancy in late sixteenth-century Switzerland, Scotland and Holland, the idea of discipline – 'the very essence of Calvinism' – began to denote the internal principles and external machinery of civil government and personal conduct. From this perspective there is a homologous relationship between curriculum and discipline: curriculum was to Calvinist educational practice as discipline was to Calvinist social practice.
>
> (Hamilton and Gibbon 1980: 14)

Hence, the evidence garnered from Paris and Glasgow in the sixteenth and seventeenth centuries can be summarised as follows in a fairly stark statement of the juxtaposition of curriculum and patterns of social control and organisation:

> The notion (was) that classes came into prominence with the rise of sequential programmes of study which in turn resonated with various Renaissance and Reformation sentiments of upward mobility. In Calvinist countries (such as Scotland) these views found their expression theologically in the doctrine of predestination (the belief that only a preordained minority could attain spiritual salvation) and, educationally, in the emergence of a national but bipartite education systems where the 'elect' (i.e. predominantly those with the ability to pay) were offered the prospect of advanced schooling, while the remainder (predominantly the rural poor) were fitted to a more conservative curriculum (like appreciation of religious knowledge and social virtue).
>
> (Hamilton 1980: 286)

In this statement one can discern some of the unique characteristics of curriculum as it developed. Alongside the power to designate what went on in classrooms, a new power emerged: the power to differentiate. We shall return to this later for, as we shall see, it was to prove of considerable significance in the construction of systems of mass schooling.

The state's involvement, sponsorship, funding and control of mass education developed first in Western Europe and this model was later utilised in patterns of national development throughout the world. 'Yet most comprehensive studies of education almost entirely overlook the historical origins of state systems of schooling... thereby ignoring the sociological significance of the successful institutionalization of this social innovation' (Ramirez and Boli 1987: 2). The state's involvement in schooling intersects crucially with the economic history of Western Europe. Whilst some of the early models for state systems pre-date the Industrial Revolution, it seems probable that the succession of the 'domestic/putter-out' system by the factory system was something of a watershed. The factory system, in breaking up existing family patterns, opened up the socialisation of the young to penetration by state systems of schooling. Yet Ramirez and Boli

(1987) stress the sheer universality of mass state-sponsored education and hence they argue that the state's compelling interest in education:

> was not solely a response to the needs of an industrialised economy, to class or status conflicts, or to unique historical conjunctures in particular countries, such as the character of the central bureaucracy in Prussia, the revolutions and reactions in France, the power of the peasantry in Sweden, or the extension of the franchise to the working classes in England.
>
> (Ramirez and Boli 1987: 2).

The common feature uniting the wide range of initiatives by states to fund and manage mass schooling was, they argue, the endeavour of constructing a national polity; the power of the nation-state, it was judged, would be unified through the participation of the state's subjects in national projects. Central to this process of socialisation and national identity was the project of mass state schooling. The sequences followed by the states that promoted this national project of mass schooling were strikingly similar. Initially there was the promulgation of a national interest in mass education; this was followed by legislation to make schooling compulsory for all. To organise the system of mass schools, state departments or Ministries of Education were formed. State authority was then exercised over all schools – both those 'autonomous' schools already existing and newly proliferating schools specifically organised or opened by the state.

As we have seen, the link between schools, and an essentially 'meritocratic' view of the social order, was discernable at the time of the Reformation. Alongside the industrialisation of Europe and the progressive embourgeoisement of society, this pattern was refined and promoted:

> with the embourgeoisement of much of European society during the nineteenth century, the significance of schooling as a general means of occupational success and social mobility became broadly institutionalised. In this way, there was an economic and social ideology that supported universal education and that complemented the political ideology of state-directed schooling for purposes of national progress. Though this 'human capital' theory of progress, which facilitated linkages between the state and school, originated among the bourgeoisie, the bourgeois classes fought against the expansion of schooling in the nineteenth century. However, the economic success of the bourgeoisie so greatly aided the organisational and extractive powers of the state that it was unable to contain the drive toward universal public education.
>
> (Ramirez and Boli 1987: 13–14)

The achievement of universal public education, specifically where organised in 'common schools', did not, however, mark the final stage in the institutionalisation of fair and equitable democratic schooling. As we have seen, the school curriculum may be employed not only to designate but also to differentiate. This power was to be substantially explored in the era of universal public education and common schooling.

In Britain (one of the first countries to industrialise) the demand for universal public education was developing considerably by the mid-nineteenth century – it formed an important plank in the populist agitations of the Chartists in the 1840s. Reviewing formal school knowledge, Bernstein (1971: 47) has argued that pedagogy, curriculum and evaluation comprise the three message systems through which formal state education is realised in the contemporary period. We have seen that the general connection between 'class' pedagogies and a curriculum based on sequence and prescription had begun to emerge earlier. In the 1850s the third prong of Bernstein's trilogy of 'message systems' began to develop, with the inauguration of the first university examination boards setting examinations for schools. The centennial report of the University of Cambridge Local Examinations Syndicate (1958: 1) states that 'the establishment of these examinations was the universities' response to petitions that they should help in the development of "schools for the middle class" '.

By the mid-nineteenth century, the feature of curriculum mentioned earlier, the power to differentiate, was being institutionalised. The birth of secondary examinations and the institutionalisation of curriculum differentiation were almost exactly contemporaneous. For instance, the Taunton Report (1868) classified secondary schooling into three grades, depending on the time spent in school. Taunton asserted that:

> The difference in time assigned makes some difference in the very nature of education itself; if a boy cannot remain at school beyond the age of 14 it is useless to begin teaching him such subjects as require a longer time for their proper study; if he can continue until 18 or 19, it may be expedient to postpone some studies that would otherwise be commenced earlier.
>
> (The Taunton Report 1868: 587)

The Taunton Report noted that 'these instructions correspond roughly but by no means exactly to the gradations of society'. In 1868, schooling until 18 or 19 years of age was reserved for the sons of men with considerable incomes independent of their own exertions, professional men, and men in business, whose profits put them on the same level. These received a mainly classical curriculum. The second grade, up age 16, was for sons of the 'mercantile classes'. Their curriculum was less classical in orientation and had a certain practical orientation. The third grade, until age 14, was for the sons of 'the smaller tenant farmer, the small tradesmen, (and) the superior artisans'. Their curriculum was based on the three 'Rs', but carried out to a very good level. These gradations cover secondary schooling. Meanwhile, most of the working class remained in elementary schools where they were taught rudimentary skills in the three 'Rs'. By this time, the curriculum functioned as a major identifier of, and mechanism for, social differentiation. This power to designate and differentiate established a conclusive place for curriculum in the epistemology of schooling.

The link with earlier religious notions of education, and indeed differentiation, can be discerned in other parts of the world. The notion of intelligence subject to 'discipline' was continuous with early Calvinist dogma. The intellect was disciplined by the moral sense and the will to carry out Christian tasks; this was not knowledge for the sake of intrinsic education, but knowledge to carry out moral and religious missions. This notion of disciplined intelligence drew on the philosophy called 'Scottish Common Sense' for its justification.

Hence, from the early Calvinist origins in Scotland notions of discipline as curriculum were carried to other parts of the world. Tomkins (1986: 35) has argued that Scottish Common Sense 'dominated philosophical thought in the English-speaking world during most of the nineteenth century and strongly influenced American college curricula'. He states that 'its influence was even stronger and more long-lasting in Canada'.

That the link between these notions of discipline and differentiation was sustained from Calvinist origins can be clearly confirmed in the work of Egerton Ryerson, the most influential architect of the Canadian public education system. Ryerson fully embraced the notion of disciplined intelligence, but for him it was crucially linked with two distinctly different types of curriculum. The first of these was essentially a preparatory level, 'requisite for the ordinary duties of life'. This curriculum comprised the study of English language and literature, mathematics, natural science and 'the outlines of mental and moral philosophy, evidences of Christianity, geography and history'. The social curriculum was devised for those planning 'professional pursuits' after going to college: in most cases, the clergy, law, politics and business. The main components of this curriculum were classics, mathematics and the physical sciences, moral science, rhetoric and *belles lettres*, and theology (Ryerson, quoted in McKillop 1979).

In the USA, the theory of mental discipline was of considerable influence in the mid-nineteenth century. But Kliebard (1986: 8) judges that by the 1890s, the theory was 'starting to unravel as a consequence of increased awareness of social transformation'. At the same time, the struggle for the American curriculum, particularly in relation to the early Republican dreams of the common school, intensified (see Franklin 1986).

In 1892, the National Education Association appointed a so-called 'Committee of Ten' to look into the issue of uniform college entrance requirements. The chairman of the committee was Charles W. Eliot, president of Harvard, an advocate of mental discipline but also a humanist with a concern for educational reform. The Report of the Committee laid down important ground rules for the school curriculum and was later seen as symptomatic of the 'crass domination exercised by the college over the high school'. In fact the domination served in time to facilitate curriculum differentiation:

> The academic subjects that the Committee saw as appropriate for the general education of all students were seen by many later reformers as appropriate only for that segment of the high school population that was destined to go on to college. In fact, subjects like French and algebra came to be called

college-entrance subjects, a term practically unknown in the nineteenth century. Even subjects like English became differentiated with standard literary works prescribed for those destined for college, while popular works and 'practical' English were provided for the majority.

(Kliebard 1986: 15–16)

The dreams of the common school were thus coming under severe strain because the Republican common core had essentially come to be viewed by some as a preparatory mode for subsequent university education. The expanding universities were thereby seen as sources of cultural property and of individual occupational mobility.

In fact, in most Western state systems of education by the end of the nineteenth century, the universities had been placed at the apex of accreditation. In some countries, like Britain, this was formalised into 'Type 1' schooling for university and professional preparation, with other types of schools for other types of people; in Canada, Egerton Ryerson promoted a belief in one curriculum for university preparation and one for 'everyday life'; and in the USA, the dream of the common school for all began to come under pressure from groups who began to develop the case for different curricula for different destinations.

But if differentiation was a growing feature of internal school curricula, it is important to assess the commonalities of mass schooling that were in evidence by the end of the nineteenth century. This is significant because certain apparent 'givens', such as school subjects, have already entered our account. We have noted that a sequencing of curriculum for 'forms' or 'classes' had emerged in the late Middle Ages and were certainly a feature of much of state schooling by the nineteenth century. A system of 'forms' or 'classes' is not, however, a classroom system. The distinction is a vital one to grasp. For instance, English public schools in the nineteenth century were often organised into 'forms' and had a formal pattern of curriculum, but there were no classrooms or subjects as such; there was not, in short, a 'classroom system'.

Hence, the public schools followed 'no common pattern of education, though they agreed on the taking of Latin and Greek as the main component of the curriculum' (Reid 1985). Each public school 'evolved its own unique form of organization with idiosyncratic vocabularies to describe them' (ibid.). The curriculum sometimes depended on the learning of common texts, but such texts might not be 'taught' in any collective manner – rather, pupils would work through them at their own individual pace. Further:

> where students were divided into 'forms' (a term referring originally to the benches on which they sat) this was done in a rough and ready manner for the convenience of teaching and not with the idea of establishing a hierarchy of ability or a sequence of learning.

(Ibid.: 296)

In the state system of schooling inaugurated in Britain in the late nineteenth century, however, a 'classroom system' was rapidly institutionalised. In a sense we can see the classroom system as a standardised invention, which essentially drives out the more idiosyncratic and individualised forms of schooling. The classroom system is, in this sense, a system for mass schooling to be administered by local and national bureaucracies.

Hamilton judges that by dawn of the twentieth century:

> the batch production rhetoric of the 'classroom system' (for example, lessons, subjects, timetables, standardisation, streaming) had become so pervasive that it successfully achieved a normative status – creating the standards against which all subsequent educational innovations came to be judged.
>
> (Hamilton 1980: 282)

In Britain, by the beginning of the twentieth century, the dominant political economy of state schooling combined the trilogy of pedagogy, curriculum and evaluation. The last piece in the trilogy was the establishment of university examination boards and here, the side effects for curriculum were to be both pervasive and long-lasting. The classroom system inaugurated a world of timetables and compartmentalised lessons; the curriculum manifestation of this systemic change was the school subject. If 'class and curriculum' entered educational discourse when schooling was transformed into a mass activity in Britain, 'classroom system and school subject' emerged at the stage at which that mass activity became a state-subsidised system. And in spite of the many alternative ways of conceptualising and organising curriculum, the convention of the subject retains its supremacy. In the modern era we are essentially dealing with the curriculum as subject.

Whilst this system was inaugurated in the 1850s, it was established on the present footing with the definition of the Secondary Regulations in 1904, which list the main subjects followed by the establishment of a subject-based 'School Certificate' in 1917. From this date, curriculum conflict began to resemble the existing situation in focusing on the definition and evaluation of examinable knowledge. Hence, the School Certificate subjects rapidly became the overriding concern of grammar schools and the academic subjects it examined soon established ascendancy in these schools' timetables. The Norwood Report (1943) stated that:

> a certain sameness in the curriculum of schools resulted from the double necessity of finding a place for the many subjects competing for time in the curriculum and the need to teach these subjects in such a way and to such a standard as will ensure success in the School Certificate examination.
>
> (The Norwood Report 1943)

The normative character of the system is clear and, as a result of 'these necessities', the curriculum had 'settled down into an uneasy equilibrium, the demands of specialists and subjects being widely adjusted and compensated' (ibid.). The extent to which university examination boards thereby influenced the curriculum through examination subjects is evident. The academic, subject-centred curriculum was in fact strengthened in the period following the 1944 Education Act. In 1951, the introduction of the General Certificate of Education allowed subjects to be taken separately at the Ordinary ('0') level (in the School Certificate, blocks of 'main' subjects had to be passed); and the introduction of an Advanced ('A') level increased subject specialisation and enhanced the link between 'academic' examinations and university 'disciplines'. The academic subjects that dominated '0' – and especially 'A' – level examinations were then closely linked to university definitions; but even more crucially, they were linked to patterns of resource allocation. Academic 'subjects' claiming close connections to university 'disciplines' were for the 'able' students. From the beginning, it was assumed that such students required 'more staff, more highly paid staff and more money for equipment and books' (Byrne 1974: 29). The crucial and sustained line between 'academic' subjects and preferential resources and status was therefore established.

But if this system was predominant with regard to staffing and resources for academic subjects in grammar schools, the implications for the other schools (and styles of curriculum) should not be forgotten. Echoing Taunton, the Norwood Report had discovered that schooling created distinctive groups of pupils, each of which needed to be treated 'in a way appropriate to itself'. This time, the social and class basis of differentiation remained the same but the rationale and mechanism for differentiation was significantly different. Before, the argument had focused on time spent at school; now the emphasis was on different 'mentalities', each recognising a different curriculum. First: 'the pupil who is interested in learning for its own sake, who can grasp an argument or follow a piece of connected reasoning'; such pupils 'educated by the curriculum commonly associated with grammar schools have entered the learned professions or have taken up higher administrative or business posts' (The Norwood Report 1943: 2). The second group, whose interests lay in the fields of applied science or applied arts, were to go to technical schools (which never developed very far). Third were the pupils who dealt 'more easily with concrete things than with ideas'; the curriculum would 'make a direct appeal to interests, which it would awaken by practical touch with affairs' (ibid.: 4); a practical curriculum, then, for a manual, occupational future.

We therefore see the emergence of a definite pattern of prioritising of pupils through curriculum; what emerges is, as I have called it elsewhere, 'the triple alliance between academic subjects, academic examinations and able pupils' (Goodson 1993: 33). Working through patterns of resource allocation, this means that a process of pervasive 'academic drift' afflicts sub-groups promoting school subjects. Hence, subjects as diverse as woodwork and metalwork, physical education, art, technical studies, bookkeeping, needlework and domestic science have pursued status improvements by arguing for enhanced academic examinations and qualifications. Likewise, schools defined as different from grammar schools – the technical schools and secondary modern schools – were ultimately drawn into the process of academic drift, both ending up competing for success through academic, subject-based styles of examination.

The conflict and compromise around the school curriculum, and within school subjects, represents at once a fragmentation and internalisation of struggles over schooling. Fragmentation, because conflicts now take place through a range of compartmentalised subjects; internalisation, because these conflicts now take place within school and subject boundaries. We shall see later how these struggles are partially expressed through, and encapsulated in, more general traditions at work within schooling.

In Britain, then, the first half of the twentieth century system saw the organisation of a state system of mass schooling, where three different types of school were built on the foundations of differentiated curriculum. The continuities since the Taunton Report of 1868 are readily discernible. In the USA, building on different origins and a distinct social structure, a different intersection of division of curriculum and division of labour can be distinguished, emerging from the original common school plan.

In their 1893 report, the Committee of Ten had specifically ruled out any preparation for 'life' or future occupations as an underpinning rationale. Their concern, as we have seen, was exclusively with academic training, in academic disciplines of study. The Committee's brief was to define a school curriculum in line with the admissions policies of the universities. We have argued that this close linking of the school curriculum to the universities left opponents of the hegemony of academic subjects (who were often also opponents of the common school) with vital ammunition. To present the common school as closely linked to universities was to implicitly leave the common school without vocational purposes beyond that of the professional preparation of the elite. This central contradiction allowed a coalition of forces to lead the attack both on the hegemonic academic curriculum and also, therefore, on the common curriculum and the common school. Hence by 1917, vocational education for occupations – for which the majority were destined – came to be seen 'as such an urgent necessity as to require federal aid' (Kliebard 1986):

> The significance of the success of vocational education was not simply that a new subject had been added, nor that a major new curriculum option had been created, but that many existing subjects, particularly at the secondary level, were becoming infused with criteria drawn from vocational education. This became evident in the increasing popularity of such courses as Business Mathematics and Business English as legitimate substitutes for traditional forms of these subjects. In very visible ways, the whole curriculum for all but the college-bound was becoming vocationalised.
>
> (Ibid.: 129)

John Dewey, at this time, immediately saw the differentiating potential of vocational education. Dewey aimed his writing against the pro-vocational writing of one of the leading advocates of vocationalising: David Snedden, Commissioner of Education in Massachusetts (and sometimes adjunct professor at Teachers' College, Columbia University). Dewey summarised Snedden's view as, 'the identification of education with acquisition of specialised skill in the management of machines at the expense of an industrial intelligence based on science and a knowledge of social problems and conditions' (Dewey 1915: 42). Dewey was clear on the effects of such vocationalism and, in a phrase echoing back to the Calvinist origins of curriculum disciplines and differentiations, argued that vocational education was likely to become 'an instrument in accomplishing the feudal dogma of social predestination' (Dewey 1916: 148). Clearly, we are a long way from the common school of the republic – and we are travelling fast in another direction, of social and cultural production and reproduction.

> Hence in the 'scant three decades' since the Committee of Ten recommendations, direct training for one's future occupational role had emerged as a major, if not the predominant, element in the high school curriculum for that segment of school population whose 'probable destiny' did not include attendance in colleges.
>
> (Kliebard 1986: 149–50)

In this sense, vocational education was 'the most successful innovation in the twentieth century' in the DSA, in that 'none other approaches it in the range of support it received and the extent to which it became implemented into the curriculum of American schools':

> On one level the success of vocational education can be attributed to the fact that it acted as a kind of magic mirror in which the powerful interest groups of the period could see their own reflected ways of reforming what was increasingly regarded as a curriculum out of tune with the times.
>
> (Ibid.: 150)

Of course this judgement is, in a sense, circular. Powerful interest groups (no doubt) particularly helped to create 'a climate of public opinion', which they could then respond to with their favoured remedy. Also, the remedy was that of only certain powerful interest groups – the universities were plainly ambivalent about the change. One would need more scholarly investigation of the views of the labour unions, immigrant and radical groups to gain an in-depth understanding of this trend. These were groups with some power at the time, and with their own associations and media. Plainly, some influential groups were more powerful than others and pursued their objectives with considerable vigour and success.

Interestingly, the American remedy differed from that in Britain and elsewhere. Vocational education was seldom pursued through separate vocational schools – the rhetoric of the common school was perhaps as important to Democratic imagery as it clearly was to the historic intentions of the founders of the American republic. Hence, the political compromise that emerged was the common school structure with differentiation internalised:

> The comprehensive high school established itself as the typical, if not the quintessential, American educational institution, with curricular tracking, both formal and informal, attending to the differentiating function that social efficiency educators considered so critical.
>
> (Ibid.: 151)

Not just social efficiency educators, it would seem, but the powerful interest groups that Kliebard mentions but fails to identify. No doubt further work in this specific area would do a great deal to elucidate the peculiar potency of social efficiency curriculum reforms. Certainly, Ross Finney's vision of the social order related to social efficiency goals was clear. The pattern of curriculum differentiation was, for him, closely akin to a pattern of social differentiation based on leadership and followership, which 'leads us again to the notion of a graduated hierarchy of intelligence and enlightenment':

> At the apex of such a system must be the experts, who are pushing forward research in highly specialised sections of the front. Behind them are such men and women as the colleges should produce, who are familiar with the findings of the experts and are able to relate part with part. By these relatively independent leaders of thought, progressive change and constant readjustment will be provided for. Back of these are the high school graduates, who are somewhat familiar with the vocabulary of those above them, have some feeling of acquaintance with the various fields, and a respect for expert knowledge. Finally, there are the duller masses, who mouth the catchwords of those in front of them, imagine that they understand, and follow by imitation.
>
> (Finney, quoted in Apple 1990: 77)

Essentially, the story of American schooling at this stage seems to be one of common purposes vitiated by internalised differentiation and subject fragmentation. This internalisation of conflict is nowhere clearer than in the internal history of school subjects. For, like the common school label, the school subject label survived – the rhetoric, at least, remained the same. For the full story, we have to open the covers and look inside. The story of the American high school curriculum is, therefore, that of a paradoxical stability of categories combined with unstable internal properties. Kliebard captures this complexity well in reviewing the struggle for the American curriculum in the years 1893–1958:

> The one fortress that proved virtually impregnable was the school subject.
>   The subject as the basic unit in the curriculum successfully resisted the more ambitious efforts to replace it with anything like functional areas of living or projects arising from student interest...
>   [...] But subject labels alone may be misleading. Some of the reforms advanced by the various interest groups were accomplished within the overall context of the subject organisation of the curriculum. To be sure, not all the changes may be regarded as signs of progress, but modest successes were achieved in restructuring, integrating and modernising the subjects that comprise the curriculum. The subjects survived but in an altered form.
>
> (Kliebard 1986: 269)

In Britain, the last 50 years of reform in schooling provide a different testimony on the fate of common school movements. For the development of the common school, the comprehensive school came late to Britain after centuries of aspiration and struggle. In 1965, the Labour government began a systematic reorganisation of the tripartite system (grammar, technical and secondary modern schools) into a unified system of comprehensive schools for all (from age 10–11 to age 16–18). My own experience as a teacher is located in this historical moment – a moment when the common school was established but had to struggle towards the achievement of a common curriculum, which alone could achieve its common purposes. From the beginning of comprehensive schools, it was possible to discern the influence of what Kliebard has called 'powerful interest groups'. For instance, the House of Commons motion that led to comprehensive reorganisation was worded this way:

> This House, conscious of the need to raise educational standards at all levels, and regretting that the realisation of this objective is impeded by the separation of children into different types of schools, notes with approval the efforts of local authorities to reorganise secondary education on comprehensive lines which will preserve all that is valuable in grammar school education for those children who now receive it and make it available to more children.
>
> (DES 1965: 1)

As we have noted, the grammar schools were essentially the gateway to the universities and to professional life. The examinations they taught towards arose out of the universities. The universities' response petitions stated that they should help in the development of 'schools for the middle classes'. Hence, the House of Commons motion pays homage to one particular tradition in British secondary schooling. The tradition for the training of the privileged minority is drawn primarily from the middle class. In phrasing the motion for the birth of the common school within this terminology, there was an implication that favouring these groups could be sustained in the common school era, but, perhaps, could now be extended to more children. But plainly a grammar school curriculum, preparing pupils for the universities and professional life, could never provide a basic common curriculum for a common school, unless of course all pupils intended to pass through university and to gain professional status. The irony of the motion had thus to be grasped as essentially a statement of obeisance to the powerful interest groups in British society. So it was to prove.

Thus, the British common school was, from the beginning, built on grounds that favoured the grammar school curriculum of the elite minority. This opened the way for internal differentiation and subject fragmentation behind the doors of the common school. As early as 1969, just four years after the House of Commons motion, a British sociologist warned that inside the common school a 'curriculum for inequality' was in action. Shipman spoke ironically of the intended convergences of curriculum development coming from the introduction of new courses into:

> a school that is still clearly divided into two sections, one geared to a system of external examinations, the other less constrained. The former is closely

tied to the universities and is within established academic traditions. The latter has a short history and is still in its formative stages.

(Shipman 1971: 101–2)

Shipman was clear that the problem was not because of the intrinsic character of the two types of curriculum, but the division into two separate sections, which 'may be producing a new means of sustaining old divisions'. Two different traditions thus produced 'two nations' of pupils:

> one is firmly planted in revered academic traditions, is adapted to teaching from a pool of factual knowledge and has clearly defined, if often irrelevant, subject boundaries. The other is experimental, looking to America rather than our own past for inspiration, focuses on contemporary problems, groups subjects together and rejects formal teaching methods. One emphasises a schooling within a framework of external examinations; the other attempts to align school work to the environment of children.

(Ibid.: 104)

But in juxtaposing the academic tradition, 'the pedagogic tradition', Shipman was leaving out a third continuing element in the British secondary school; it was not only to 'align school work to the environment of the child', as there had always been a utilitarian tradition concerned with preparing children for the environment of work. This utilitarian strain was, we noted, the tendency that, under the guise of vocational education, helped to shatter the notion of unified purpose in the American common school. So in Britain, it became the focus of those concerned with the results of the comprehensive school. It was in fact a Labour Prime Minister – James Callaghan – who, in 1976, masterminded a 'great debate' on education. The priorities became clear in a speech he gave in October 1976, at Ruskin College (Oxford): 'No new policies were proposed but the government had now established that educational standards, and the relationship of education to the economy, were to be as much of a priority as comprehensive reform in solution' (Callaghan 1976). Hence a decade after its inception, the comprehensive reform of schooling was placed alongside the need for education to serve the economy.

In the following decade any question of equal concern for comprehensive reform and education for the economy rapidly vanished. With the election of Margaret Thatcher in 1979, the comprehensive idea came under attack from a variety of sources – but again, the need for more vocational education was the main rationale provided for confirming internal differentiation. The government launched a Technical and Vocational Initiative, funded by central government, to restructure the internal curriculum of the secondary schools. In addition, an Assisted Places Scheme was funded to sponsor private and direct grant schools, traditionally the preserve of the middle and upper classes. In the latter school the traditional academic curriculum predominated, whilst in the state schools more vocational education was rapidly pursued. The British experience reads in certain specific ways like a rapidly compressed re-run of the history of the American common school. Powerful interest groups have sought to erode the possibility of the common school and to reestablish and enhance differentiation through the promotion of vocational initiatives.

In Britain the history of secondary schooling may now be returning full circle, with moves to develop academies, academy chains and free schools. Significantly, the National Curriculum, which has been legislated for the public sector schools, has not been extended to the private 'public schools'. Again, as is happening in different ways in the United States, this is taking place alongside a reconstitution of the social configuration of schooling. The school subject provides a microcosm wherein the history of the social forces, which underpin the patterns of curriculum and schooling, might be scrutinised and analysed.

References

Apple, M.W. (1990) *Ideology and Curriculum*, 2nd edition, New York and London: Routledge.

Bernstein, B. (1971) 'On the Classification and Framing of Educational Knowledge', in M.F.D. Young (ed.) *Knowledge and Control*, London: Macmillan.

Boli, J. (1989) *New Citizens for a New Society: The Institutional Origins of Mass Schooling in Sweden*, Oxford: Pergamon Press.

Byrne, E.M. (1974) *Planning and Educational Inequality*, Slough: NFER.

Callaghan, J., the Rt. Hon. Prime Minister (1976) Speech, 18 October, Oxford, Ruskin College.

DES (1965) 'Organization of secondary education', *Circular* 10/65, London: HMSO.

Dewey, J. (1915) 'Education vs. trade training – Dr Dewey's reply', *The New Acpaslic*, 3, 42.

Dewey, J. (1916) *Democracy and Education 1946: An Introduction to the Philosophy of Education*, New York: Macmillan.

Franklin, B. (1986) *Building the American Community*, London, New York and Philadelphia: Falmer Press.

Goodson, I.F. (1993) *School Subjects and Curriculum Change*, London, New York and Philadelphia: Falmer Press.

Hamilton, D. (1980) 'Adam Smith and the moral economy of the classroom system', *Journal of Curriculum Studies*, 12, 4.

Hamilton, D. and Gibbons, M. (1980) 'Notes on "the origins of the educational terms class and curriculum"', paper presented at American Educational Research Association: Boston.

Kliebard, H.M. (1986) *The Struggle for the American Curriculum 1893–1958*, Boston and London: Routledge and Kegan Paul.

McKillop, A.B. (1979) *A Disciplined Intelligence*, Montreal: McGill Queens University Press.

Norwood Report, The (1943) 'Board of education: curriculum and examinations in secondary schools', report of the Committee, Chairman Sir Cyril Norwood, of the Secondary School Examination Council, 23 June, London: HMSO.

Ramirez, F.O. and Boli, J. (1987) 'The political construction of mass schooling: European origins and worldwide institutionalism', *Sociology of Education*, 60, 2–17.

Reid, W.A. (1985) 'Curriculum Change and the Evolution of Educational Constituencies: The English Sixth Form in the Nineteenth Century', in I.F. Goodson (ed.) *Social*

Histories of the Secondary Curriculum: Subjects for Study, London and Philadelphia: Falmer Press.

Shipman, M. (1971) 'Curriculum for Inequality', in R. Hooper (ed.) *The Curriculum: Context, Design and Development*, Edinburgh: Oliver and Boyd.

Taunton Report, The (1868) 'Schools Inquiry Commission'. Available at: http://books. google.co.uk/books?id=n7yLL47MUKQC&pg=PA89&lpg=PA89&dq=taunton+report +1868&source=bl&ots=7WDZ-TqN3U&sig=fOEDmnG8QQ8Sz_sY87kyl- YRDjc&hl=en&sa=X&ei=tn_vUuWHFcmshQfe8oGQCw&ved=0CGQQ6AEwBg#v=o nepage&q=taunton%20report%201868&f=false (accessed on 7 February 2014).

Tomkins, G.O. (1986) *A Common Countenance: Stability and Change in the Canadian Curriculum*, Scarborough, Ontario: Prentice Hall.

University of Cambridge Local Examinations Syndicate (1958) Centennial Report, Cambridge.

3   Times of educational change

Towards an understanding of patterns of historical and cultural refraction

In this chapter, I report some of the findings from a four-year study of educational reforms in 8 European countries, which was undertaken for the European Commission. The countries covered are: England, Ireland, Portugal, Spain, Finland, Sweden and Greece, and the research was conducted from 2004–8.[1]

The aim of the Professional Knowledge project (PROFKNOW 2002–8) was to seek to understand how plans for educational reform and restructuring impinged on patterns of professional knowledge, with particular regard to teaching and health professionals (nurses and doctors).

In this chapter, I concentrate primarily on the education sector. The methodological basis of the research is fairly complex, as would be expected in a multidisciplinary, multinational study, but the full methodological armoury can be reviewed at the PROFKNOW website.

Broadly, the research study employed a narrative approach to studying two kinds of narratives. First, what were called 'systemic narratives': these comprised the main documentary sources of the restructuring and reform initiatives in each national and regional area. To bring this closer to the educational settings, however, these systemic narratives were juxtaposed against what were called 'work–life narratives'. Work–life narratives focused on life history interviews with a range of teachers employed in schools – primarily secondary schools – in the national settings. Where possible, the life history interviews covered a cohort plan so that the different generations of teachers were given a chance to develop their narratives according to the historical period in which they had worked. Cohorts therefore covered three broad time spans: teachers who had begun work in the 1960s and 1970s; those who had begun work in the 1980s and 1990s; and those who had recently begun work.

The two sections that follow review systemic narratives in relation to particular historical periods and the second section looks at teachers' work–life narratives in relationship to these systemic reforms.

Historical periods and systemic narratives

Our work on studying generations, as originally planned, led us to conceptualise historical periods of restructuring. The work uses the French historical methodology developed by the *Annaliste* school of historians. They focus on particular *conjunctures*, where broad-based restructuring is promoted. It is possible to identify particular historical periods where maximal windows of opportunity for broad-based restructuring exist (for an extended commentary on historical periodisation and education, see Goodson 2005).

For this reason it is crucial, when dealing with educational transitions and reform initiatives, to identify and understand historical periodisation and its conceptual and methodological limitations. The definition of periods allows us to define the possibility for professional action and professional narratives at particular points in historical time. In the PROFKNOW project, we have found that the capacities for action and narrative construction differ greatly according to the historical periods studied. Moreover, we can begin to see how each country, and in some cases each region, has different systemic 'trajectories'. These historical trajectories mean that the process of restructuring approaches each state or region from, so to speak, a different angle. Historical periods and systemic trajectories can both be seen as 'refracting' centralised restructuring initiatives. Studying translation and diffusion gives us access to the processes of refraction.

Because of the complexity of historical periodisation, we asked each national team to prepare their own historical analysis. This periodisation tells us important facts about changes in education and health care in their respective national contexts. But they also tell us about the manner in which different national teams organise their ways of dealing with these state institutions. Their perceptions of welfare state developments are themselves, therefore, periodised.

We enclose a summary chart of these perceptions. Although we have employed the term 'dictatorship' in the southern European cases, our national team referred rather to internal 'transitions' within those periods and to growing patterns of modernisation.

Nonetheless, the late evolution of welfare states in the south stands in sharp juxtaposition to the post-war social democracies in the north. Sweden, Finland and England see fast expansion after 1945, but England and Ireland move rapidly into reform mode through the 1980s. This neo-liberal style of restructuring then becomes a broad-based movement across all 8 countries in the 1990s, but builds on sharply different trajectory foundations (see Table 3.1).

These rather basic definitions of periodisation nonetheless serve some general purposes. They show a clear distinction between the southern European states and the northern states, with regard to their historical trajectories. In the southern nation-states, dictatorship came to an end in the mid 1970s and 'welfare state' patterns slowly began to emerge. At, more or less, the same time in the north, established welfare states were coming under pressure to marketise and reform. England and Ireland led this neo-liberal agenda pattern of restructuring in the 1980s; other countries began the same agenda in the 1990s (see Table 3.2).

Hence, when that which Meyer calls the 'world movement' of neo-liberal educational reforms started in all countries in the 1990s, it began on very different historical foundations. The historical trajectories of each nation-state effectively

Table 3.1 Periodisation in national contexts

National Case	Periods	
England	1945–79	progressive narrative on welfare state expansion
	1979–97	marketisation narrative
	1997–2007	narrative of the middle way: targets, tests and tables
Finland	1945–69	preparatory phase: building the welfare state
	1970–89	the golden age
	1990–2007	restructuring
Greece	1945–67	post-war period
	1967–74	dictatorship
	1975–89	welfare state building
	1991–2007	restructuring
Ireland	1970–86	the demise of apprenticeship and increasing secularisation
	1987–97	envisioning the future partnership: a new approach
	1997–2007	opening the floodgates of reform
Portugal	1945–74	dictatorship
	1974–6	revolutionary period
	1977–85	normalisation
	1985–2007	restructuring
Spain	1939–76	dictatorship
	1977–90	normalisation
	1990–2000	welfare state building
	2000–2007	restructuring
Sweden	1945–75	welfare state expansion: services for all
	1975–92	decentralisation and deregulation
	1992–2000	marketisation
	2000–7	quality agenda

Source: Goodson and Lindblad (2010).

reformulate and refract this neo-liberal reform agenda in starkly different ways. This is reflected in the juxtaposition of these systemic narratives to teachers' work–life narratives in each country.

Before we review the work–life narratives, it may be worth providing the PROFKNOW report summary of neo-liberal reform initiatives. The following summary is drawn from Beach's work on the PROFKNOW project and accords with much of the research work characterising this period of restructuring (e.g. Ball 2007).

Of course, restructuring of systems is not achieved by the enunciation of policy discourse; restructuring works only in association with teachers' work–life narratives and practices.

We have seen that neo-liberal reforms constituted a world movement and delineated some of the key characteristics of the world movement in the current conjuncture. This conjuncture was discerned earlier, when we looked at historical

Table 3.2 The main features of public service restructuring in the case studies

- decentralisation
- development of an emphatic discourse of privatisation and marketisation (habituation)
- standardisation of instruction and assessment
- sacrifice of the critical mission of professional education/training to practical and technical training in economic interests
- conversion of public services to private
- business takeover of education and care supply and teacher and nursing supply
- creation of quasi markets for consolidating the processes of privatisation
- authorities forming agencies for contracting out services to private suppliers
- costs of administration shifted from costs of public ownership and control to costs of managing and monitoring outsourced delivery
- increased costs from franchise effects (un/under-employment) on public employees
- the increased objectification of labour and increases in the value form of labour
- dissemination of a view of learners and care recipients as economically rational, self-interested individuals and the reconstruction of supply in line with this vision
- redefinition of democracy in terms of consumer choice
- increased objectification of teachers and nurses, learners and patients, care and curricula and (increasingly) professional education and educators as factors of production
- creation of a labour buffer (surplus army of labour) in the education and care sectors at the same time as (at least in some education sectors) posts are increasingly difficult to fill and notoriously difficult to maintain continuity in
- increased class differences in terms of education and care supply and consumption, i.e. in terms of who provides care and to/for whom
- increased inequalities in service work conditions
- increases in quick training programmes to maximise economic gains
- increases in judgement of performances according to consumer values

Source: Goodson and Lindblad (2010).

periodisation. With growing force in the 8 countries in the 1980s, this became a generalised movement in the mid 1990s.

Crucially however, we saw how the restructuring of educational systems in European nation-states builds on different trajectory foundations and historical periodisation. There turned out to be critical zones of refraction in understanding how restructuring initiatives are translated and diffused in a specific milieu.

Work–life narratives

We discern a range of responses when juxtaposing systemic narratives and work–life narratives. In the next section we provide examples from most of our case study countries. But this should not be taken to mean that countries react monolithically to restructuring initiatives. There are a variety of 'points of refraction' or milieu membranes through which restructuring policies must pass: national systems, regional systems, school board systems – right through to individual

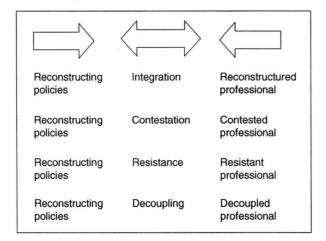

Figure 3.1 Differentiated strategic responses to the juxtaposition of systemic and work–life narratives

Source: Goodson and Lindblad (2010).

schools and individual classrooms and teachers. This means that a wide range of responses is possible, even if certain national characteristics of response can be evidenced.

Figure 3.1 provides a framework for analysing the various main configurations found when juxtaposing systems' narratives and teachers' and nurses' work–life narratives.

A number of national case studies highlight the different juxtapositions but, as noted, this is not to argue that national responses are monolithic. The English case study, for instance, finds compelling evidence of integration and of restructuring affecting professional change towards what we call 're-framed' professionals. The report notes that:

> Teachers and nurses are trapped in the gap between government rhetoric and political narratives about choices and entitlements and the reality of the classroom or the hospital situation.
>
> The interviews highlight the unease of professionals with overriding national policies. Using choice and competition as methods of raising standards in public services is seen as intrinsically contradictory and causing greater inequalities in society and taking professionals away from the aims of putting clients first. However, the lack of a national underlying oppositional ideology (with socialism having been dropped by the Labour Party) leads to inward motivation and increased professional localism.
>
> (PROFKNOW 2003)

England poses an interesting case, given the historical periods and trajectories we have evidenced earlier. One of the countries to build up a strong welfare state after 1945, England became a leader in neo-liberal restructuring initiatives aimed at transforming, if not dismantling, this welfare system. In Sweden and Finland, the welfare system has proved more durable and politically sustainable. Hence both the Swedish and Finnish studies show how restructuring has been contested and often, if attempted, sidestepped by professionalism:

> The slogan 'personality is the most important instrument of work' is predominant among Finnish teachers, indeed the practising teachers emphasise that the long science-based teacher education, except practical training periods, provides only a theoretical foundation for professional work. For them the most important source of knowledge is the practical activities, common sense, everyday experiences and learning by doing. In addition, personal hobbies and activities outside the school are valued as well. Indeed, according to some recent studies the opportunities to draw on personal interests and to exercise independent judgement are among the most important motivations for being a teacher.
>
> (Ibid.)

This example is common in the established welfare societies of Sweden and Finland, as it once was in England. The belief in professional autonomy, motivating and creative, leads to loosely coupled or decoupled restructuring strategies. Significantly, Finland, where professional autonomy is deeply entrenched and restructuring policies are least intensive, produces highly successful educational indicators. This appears to be an efficient and motivated professional system, which builds on a belief in professional expertise, judgement and commitment. Without these elements it is difficult to see restructuring working smoothly, however intensive and politically promoted it might be.

Certainly restructuring has the features of a world movement that political elites are promoting, but we can see how the different historical periodisations and trajectories crucially *refract* this process. In Sweden and Finland, deeply entrenched systems of social democracy and professional expertise appear to have more enduring leverage than in England and Ireland.

Now let us turn to the very different historical periodisations and trajectories in southern Europe. As we noted, these countries (Portugal, Spain and Greece) came late to welfare systems and social democracy. Hence the restructuring world movement enters these societies at a different stage and, so to speak, at a different angle. The result of this trajectory of engagement is clear in the way that restructuring initiatives are refracted.

In Portugal, contestation and resistance seem endemic. The report is eloquent and very clear:

> The strategies developed by the teaching profession have been mainly reactive: they express mostly a systematic rejection of the initiatives proposed by

the central administrator than a proactive and anticipatory presentation of new forms of structuring and promoting the professional group.... Only recently (since the end of the 1980s) have the unions discussed a structure for the teaching career, but even then, they have done so ... in a primarily reactive manner, trying to keep things the way they were and resisting any attempts to change, rather than proposing structural changes that might improve the quality of professional practice and its outcomes.

(Ibid.)

This Portuguese response shows how the role of periods and trajectories is a vital conceptual tool in understanding how restructuring initiatives are received by professional groups; received and then refracted. The periodisations and trajectories in Greece have considerable similarities and, for the older generation who knew the revolutionary period, can be clearly evidenced. Here, though, generational restrictions can more clearly be drawn than was the case in Portugal, where generational conformity seems more substantial:

Generational differences in the professional strategies towards restructuring are expressed as differentiated attitudes towards intensification of working conditions.

Senior teachers and nurses tend to ignore the pressures and they use experience and collegial learning as the main way to cope with new demands at work and compensation for the lack of up-to-date knowledge. Working conditions are experienced as more intense and pressurising on the part of the middle-aged teachers. Hierarchies among this age group are more peculiar since their formal qualifications vary substantially (some of them having two years initial education, some others four years plus additional university 'equation' training). Younger teachers and nurses tend to come from a richer socioeconomic background and they all have university qualifications. They experience restructuring not as part of historical consciousness regarding the transitions the profession is undergoing but as a frustrating client-oriented working environment. Personnel shortages add to this feeling.

Substantial generational differences refer to the confidence in syndicalism as an effective professional strategy. In both the teaching and the nursing professions, the older generation is aware of the contribution of collective action in proposing and defending professional strategies. However, the younger generation of nurses and teachers are not interested in syndicalism and do not become active members partly because the image of syndicalism has faded as part of the more general mistrust in politics.

(Ibid.)

The Spanish case study is a beautifully constructed analysis of some of the complexities and refractions of restructuring when viewed from below at the local level. Their analysis confirms the essential point about periodisation and trajectories and generations:

Talking about restructuring both in education and in health requires us to talk briefly about structuring. As we have already said, the very late development of the welfare state in Spain has to be acknowledged when dealing with restructuring. Only doing this one can understand the specificity of the Spanish case, which is something like a compressed and anomalous history of the welfare state in Europe. Public health and education institutions were firstly developed in democracy in the 1990s. Before that, as we know, there were timid build-ups by Franco's regime. Up until 1967 in health and 1970 in education there was not a comprehensive system for providing basic services to most citizens. So basically what we see during the 1990s is the building of the kind of welfare institutions that most European countries developed after the Second World War. A decade later, the first clear symptoms of their dismantling were manifest.

(Ibid.)

The report shows responses that are quite like aspects of the Portuguese and Greek (certainly older generation) work–life narratives.

The recent history of the Spanish educational system just mentioned provided a quite concrete picture of restructuring from a system's narrative. However, it failed to be identified as a meaningful player for the teachers themselves. A high degree of scepticism and cynicism was observed regarding the impact of policies in everyday practices. First, our evidence shows that the Spanish teachers we studied perceive their profession and their work on a daily, personal basis rather than as embedded in large socio-political contexts. Therefore, restructuring was not thought of as a kind of local expression of global dynamics; so a very interesting gap remains between their conception of the system and the theoretical causes and explanations some theorists of the field may put forward. Even when explicitly drawing attention to the changes in legislation from our side, this was not perceived as influencing day-to-day business, either because changes are too cosmetic or because they lack the necessary time to become applied practice. The educational projects associated with the different political parties were met with a dismissive shrug, and were considered to be unable to affect working conditions for the better. What happens on the level of politics is perceived as having little or nothing to do with real necessities in the school:

> Sophia: I don't care about a lot of political things, but in your daily life.... That's also why I believe a little less each day in political things. I mean, the little I know, they disappoint me so much that beyond my daily life, why should I care about politics?
>
> (Ibid.)

Rosa's view is similar:

> In her eyes it is not that the actual laws don't function but rather that they are missing the necessary resources to be actually implemented.
>
> (Ibid.)

The Spanish case points to the conceptual complexity of professional responses and highlights the differences between the teachers noted above (and nurses) and between diverse local settings. Their warning is important: a health warning against conceptual over-generalisation.

By comparing our cases, it becomes apparent how varied and often contradictory processes of 'restructuring' are. They comprise many facets, temporalities and scales.

Thus it is clear how historical periods and trajectories operate in identifiable ways to refract restructuring initiatives. We have clear evidence that the main responses delineated in the earlier chart of restructuration, contestation, resistance and decoupling can be found in our case studies. Moreover, our work on generational periodisation and trajectories is of some utility in understanding the pattern of responses.

Theory is always of specific rather than general use. We too need to be parsimonious with our general ambitions. But if there is a message to those in governing agencies who sponsor restructuring initiatives, it would be to advise a similar caution in promoting over-centralised, over-generalised expectations and edicts. We have seen how a world movement like restructuring has been widely promoted in Europe. We have also seen how the response has varied immensely and how sensitivity to generations, periodisation and national trajectories helps explain the process of 'refraction'.

At the end point of the multi-layered refraction process sits the individual or professional. Still, we should remember a key player – probably the key player – in the process. Alienate your professional groups and your restructuring rhetoric will remain just that – political rhetoric. Let us end, then, with the recognition of the central and inestimable value of the professional contribution of teachers and nurses in the actual delivery of that about which the rest of us pronounce. The professional teacher was described in this way by an experienced Finnish teacher educator, and we should remember Finland's exemplary performance in education:

> Good teacherhood is a personal quality, not a skill learnable by heart. Already at the classroom door one could see if the teacher trainee had enough charisma, enthusiasm, aura and know-how. That was completed by an easy and respectful attitude towards the pupils. Theory could not help if the sentiment was wrong.
>
> (Ibid.)

Indeed, theory could not help if the sentiment was wrong – neither, one is tempted to add, could restructuring if the antecedent trajectory or professional sentiment is wrong.

Conclusion

Alongside this report of empirical findings, I have provided some speculative comments on patterns of historical refraction. In these instances, refraction refers to the capacity for global patterns to be redirected and reordered by their setting in historical periods and cultural contexts. Just as with the refraction of light through a window, global initiatives that follow similar intentions and directions can end up moving in unintended directions and sequences. Whilst, in some ways, refraction is similar to the concept of re-contextualisation, the work focuses not only on the external changes in local and professional cultures and in personal contexts, but also on internal changes in perceptions and narratives. As well as the 'external relations' of change, therefore, we try to elicit evidence of the 'internal affairs' of change.

In terms of a focus on new capitalism, it is perhaps instructive to reflect that the economic profession itself is highly subject to refraction. Fourcade's recent study, *Economists and Societies: Discipline and Profession in the United States, Britain and France, 1980s–1990s* (2009), provides a historical and sociological study of the developments of the economist professional discourse in three countries.

Basically, she argues that within each nation a distinctive professional culture has developed. In the USA, this is characterised by a unique federal structure, in which relationships with the state are held at bay by the traditions of autonomy in universities and economic departments. This makes for a profoundly different pattern to that found in France and the UK. In France, the economists are more immersed in the culture of the state and are characterised as public administrators trained and educated in the *grand corps d'état*. In Britain, the elitist pattern of economist training comes from an amalgam of Oxbridge training and the institutional infrastructure of the Government, the civil service and the major London banks.

Thus, whilst in some ways the new capitalism poses similar questions for economists studying the new world order, each nation's economists pursue this from a different historical and political trajectory. Hence 'despite all the talk about globalisation, each country wants to find economic solutions that suit its historical paths and conditions' (Hess 2009: 54).

This pursuit of national solutions can be seen in the PROFKNOW report. Broadly, the English and Irish have pursued the neo-liberal agenda in the fastest and deepest manner. More recently, in the southern European countries, with their less well-established social democratic structures, we see 'the market' driving towards an abandonment of these visions; though the result on the front line of education is less coherent or conclusive. In the most historically grounded social democratic systems of Sweden and Finland, the response has been more in line with a vision of trusting professionals and, most clearly in the Finnish case, underpinning 'good teacherhood' and professional judgement.

Since neo-liberalism has pushed transparency over accountability and educational results, it seems strange that they have not drawn any lessons from the PISA study of educational standards.[2] These show, with deafening clarity, that those countries that have pursued neo-liberal reforms in the fastest and deepest manner, such as England, perform very poorly in educational standards. Meanwhile, those that have defended a social democratic vision and have explicitly valued professional autonomy, such as Finland, have produced top-rate educational standards. It would seem time to seriously scrutinise the neo-liberal orthodoxy in the field of education.

Notes

1   This chapter was presented at the JEP25 Seminar, 'Education, Capitalism and Crisis' at the Institute of Education, 24 June 2010.
2   The Programme for International Student Assessment (PISA) is a triennial international survey which aims to evaluate education systems worldwide by testing the skills and knowledge of 15-year-old students. To date, students representing more than 70 countries and economies have participated in the assessment. See www.oecd.org/pisa/aboutpisa/ (accessed 13 November 2013).

References

Ball, S.J (2007) *Education Plc: Private Sector Participation in Public Sector Education*, London: Routledge.

Fourcade, M. (2009) *Economists and Societies: Discipline and Profession in the United States, Britain, and France, 1980s–1990s*, Princeton: Princeton University Press.

Goodson, I.F. (2005) 'The Long Waves of Reform', in *Learning, Curriculum and Life Politics*, pp. 105–29. London and New York: Routledge.

Goodson, I.F. and Lindblad, S. (eds) (2010) *Professional Knowledge and Educational Restructuring in Europe*. Rotterdam, Boston and Taipei: Sense.

Hess, A. (2009) 'The backstory of the credit crunch', *Times Higher Education*, December 17, p. 24.

PROFKNOW (2002–8) Professional Knowledge in Education and Health, 'Restructuring Work and Life Between State and Citizens in Europe', UK: University of Brighton, Sweden: University of Gothenburg, Athens: National and Kopodistorian, Finalnd: University of Joensuu, Spain: University of Barcelona, Portugal: University of the Azores, Ireland: St Patrick's College, Dublin City University, Sweden: University of Stockholm. Available at: www.ips.gu.se/english/Research/research_programmes/pop/current_research/PROFKNOW/ (accessed 6 September 2013).

4 Curriculum as narration
Tales from the children of the colonised

with Ruth Deakin Crick

Introduction

In this chapter we focus on the role of narrative as a core pedagogical tool in inquiry-based learning. Somewhat neglected in learning theory, narrative provides us with a tool for what Bauman describes as 'the unfamiliar task of theorising a formative process which is not guided from the start by the target form, designed in advance' (2001: 139). Contemporary explorations in inquiry-based learning seek to engage the learner in a formative process of problem formulation and solving, but necessarily do so in a context where the dominant metaphor is curriculum as prescription, rather than curriculum as narration; where the process of learning is predetermined by the curriculum and assessment requirements and knowledge is pre-packaged in particular subject areas, or disciplines. This inevitably marginalises narrative ways of knowing, and those students and communities (such as Indigenous Australian communities) where this is a primary way of knowing and learning. The approach to inquiry-based learning, discussed by Deakin Crick in a special issue of *Curriculum Journal* (Deakin Crick 2009), rehabilitates the role of narrative in learning, and it does so in three distinct modes. First, there is the life narrative of the learner; second, the narratives of the particular community of which the learner is a part; and third, the narratives embedded and uncovered by the learner in the process of co-constructing knowledge. Our argument is that when the three horizons of these narratives coalesce in a learning project, then the learning that takes place is personal, transformative and enduring. Not only is the learner constructing new knowledge in response to a particular problem – in an outcome that is measurable in the usual way – but, in doing so, she or he is narrating their own story through the curriculum. There has been a shift to curriculum as narration. Before exploring this further, with examples, we first look at the challenges of curriculum as prescription.

Curriculum as prescription

In his recent writing on education, Zygmun Bauman has drawn attention to the work of Margaret Mead and her life companion, Gregory Bateson. Mead said that:

The Social Structure of a society and the way learning is structured – the way it passes from mother to daughter, from father to son, from mother's brother to sister's son, from shaman to novice, from mythological specialists to explained specialists – determine far beyond the actual content of the learning both how individually we will learn to think and how the store of learning, the sum total of separate pieces of skill and knowledge … is shared and used.

(Mead 1964: 79)

Gregory Bateson also wrote some fascinating work on learning. Learning, in his analysis, divides into three linked but distinct types. There is the primary learning, 'first-degree' learning of content, which is then remembered and repeated. Then there is *'deutero'* learning: what we might call secondary learning, the subterranean process of learning to learn. Bauman says that this secondary learning 'depends not so much on the diligence and talents of the learners and the competence and assiduity of their teachers, as on the attributes of the world in which the former pupils are bound to live their lives' (Bauman 2001: 24). Tertiary learning he summarises as learning: 'how to break the regularity, how to rearrange fragmentary experiences into heretofore unfamiliar patterns' (Bauman 2001: 125). Tertiary learning is about living without habits and routinised learning; it's about breaking away from pre-digested prescriptions of curriculum and moving to the definition, ownership and ongoing narration of our own curriculum.

Looking at these three types of learning highlights the current crisis of curriculum and of educational studies generally. The old patterns of curriculum development and curriculum study are utterly unsuited to the new society of risk, instability and rapid change in which we now live. They are locked into primary learning and prescription. Bauman says:

I suggest that the overwhelming feeling of crises experienced by philosophers, theorists and practitioners of education alike … have little to do with the faults, errors or negligence of the professional pedagogue or failures of educational theory, but quite a lot to do with the universal melting of identities with the deregulation and privatization of the identity – formation processes, the dispersal of authorities, the polyphony of the messages and ensuing fragmentation of life which characterizes the world we live in.

(Bauman 2001: 127)

Bauman, then, is clear that the crisis of curriculum is not an internal matter, a question of failures of practice or research – it is a broad question of positionality: people, and in this instance curriculum people, are searching for solutions in the wrong place. Rather than writing new prescriptions for schools – new curriculum or new reform guidelines – they need to question the very validity of pre-digested prescriptions typical of our formal 'curricula' in a world of flux and change. We need, in short, to move from curriculum as prescription to curriculum as identity narration, from prescribed cognitive learning to life management narrative learning.

It is this shift that we will try to outline in this chapter. First, we will deal with the redundancy of curriculum as prescription and, second, we will tentatively outline the move to curriculum as narrative, which we believe marks the way to our new social future. We will do this drawing on data from a project with Indigenous young people in a school in New South Wales. Indigenous communities are perhaps amongst those who 'feel the pain the most' in relation to this crisis of curriculum, partly because Indigenous ways of knowing are rooted in narrative and relationship but also because the legacy of dispossession and colonisation has left them marginalised in terms of the erstwhile social and economic benefits of curriculum as prescription. Their voices in this study give high definition to the practice of curriculum as narration, in a manner that may, ironically, give something important back to Western education systems.

First, we discuss the established practice of curriculum as prescription on which so many of the assumptions of practitioners and researchers are based. The primacy of the ideology of curriculum as prescription can be evidenced in even a cursory glimpse at curriculum literature. This view of curriculum develops from a belief: that we can dispassionately define the main ingredients of the course of study, and then proceed to teach the various segments and sequences in systematic turn. Despite the obvious simplicity – not to say crudity – of this view, the 'objectives game' is still, if 'not the only game in town', then certainly the main game. There may be many reasons for this continuing predominance, but explanatory potential is not, we think, one of the factors.

Curriculum as prescription supports important mystiques about state schooling and society. Most notably, it supports the mystique that expertise and control reside within central government, educational bureaucracies or the university community. Providing nobody exposes this mystique, the worlds of 'prescription rhetoric' and 'schooling as practice' can co-exist. Both sides benefit from such peaceful co-existence. The agencies of curriculum as prescription are seen to be 'in control' and the schools are seen to be 'delivering' and can carve out a good degree of autonomy if they accept the rules and win by them. Curriculum prescriptions thereby set certain parameters, with transgression and occasional transcendence being permissible as long as the rhetoric of prescription and management is not challenged. Those who do not thrive within this type of curriculum provision are further marginalised.

Of course there are 'costs of complicity' in accepting the myth of prescription: above all these involve, in various ways, acceptance of established modes of power relations. Perhaps most importantly, the people intimately connected with the day-to-day social construction of curriculum and schooling – the teachers – are thereby effectively disenfranchised in the 'discourse of schooling'. They become 'deliverers' of content and technicians for the production of predetermined assessment outcomes. To continue to exist, their power to diagnose, create and facilitate personalised learning opportunities must basically remain unspoken and unrecorded. This, then, is the price of complicity.

With regard to the study of curriculum, the 'costs of complicity' are ultimately catastrophic. The historic compromise we have described has led to the displacement of a whole field of study. It has led to the directing of scholarship into fields which service the mystique of central and/or bureaucratic control. For scholars who benefit from maintaining this mystique – in the universities particularly – this complicity is, to say the least, self-serving (for more on this argument, see Goodson 2005).

Prescription and the establishment of power make easy allies. As Goodson (1995) argued, the curriculum was basically invented as a concept to direct and control the teacher's licence and potential freedom in the classroom. Over the years, the alliance between prescription and power has been carefully nurtured so that curriculum becomes a device to reproduce existing power relations in society. The children of powerful, resourceful parents enjoy curriculum inclusion and the less advantaged suffer from curriculum exclusion. As Bourdieu (2000) has argued, a parent's 'cultural capital' effectively buys success for their student offspring in this way. One of the most significant curriculum building blocks of schooling, which operates as a device for social exclusion, is the 'traditional school subject'.

Exclusive pursuits: the invention of school subjects

The central place of 'academic' subjects is ensconced in Western schools and so, therefore, is an in-built pattern of social prioritising and exclusion (Layton 1973; Goodson 1993; Goodson 1995). School subjects are defined not in a disinterested scholastic way, but in close relationship to the power and interests of social groups. The more powerful the social group, the more likely they are to exercise power over school knowledge. School subject groups tend to move progressively away from social relevance or vocational emphasis. High status in the secondary school tends to focus on abstract theoretical knowledge divorced from the workaday world or the everyday world of the learner. To these high-status academic subjects go the main resources in our school systems: the better-qualified teachers, the favourable sixth form ratios and the students deemed most able. The link is now strengthened by New Labour initiatives in terms of targets, tests and league tables. In this way a pattern of social prioritising, built on exclusive pursuits, found itself at the heart of a programme of social inclusion. Such a central contradiction and a range of other exclusionary devices, inherited unknowingly or unthinkingly, have contributed to the failure of New Labour policies to further social inclusion.

The underpinning prioritisation of academic school subjects effectively strangled new attempts to develop a more inclusive curriculum in comprehensive schools. This pattern of social prioritising was finally consolidated in the new 'National Curriculum' of 1988, which almost exactly re-established Morant's Secondary Regulations of 1904 – The Public School and Grammar School Curriculum was firmly reinstated. A pattern of subject knowledge based on selective exclusion became the lynchpin of the curricula to be offered in comprehensive schools.

Curriculum as prescription and powerful interest groups are locked in a potent historical partnership, which structures curriculum in basic ways and effectively subverts any passing innovations or reforms. The prescriptions provide clear 'rules of the game' for schooling and finance and resources are tied into these rules. Curriculum research, with a few honourable exceptions, has also tended to follow the 'rules of the game' by accepting curriculum as prescription as its starting point even when, in the odd case, advocating resistance or transformation.

The reason for hope now comes because, although the rules of the game for curriculum and for reproducing the social order are well established, the wider social order and associated rules of the game are now undergoing seismic change. This will destabilise the cosy alliance of power and prescription in unpredictable but definitive ways. The curriculum game is about to experience pulverising change but often seems blissfully unaware of what the future holds. In the new era of flexible work organisation, workers face unpredictable and constantly changing assignments:

> The types of skills required to practise flexible occupations do not on the whole demand long-term and systematic learning. More often than not, they transform a well-profiled logically coherent body of skills and habits from the asset it used to be, into the handicap it is now.
>
> (Bauman 2001: 132)

Long-established and prescribed courses of study therefore become a handicap to the new flexible work order. Curriculum as prescription might provide residual patterns of social reproduction, but its increasingly economic dysfunctionality calls its continuity into question by powerful economic interests and global pressures. Bauman described the dilemma with exquisite precision and with utter clarity for our curriculum futures:

> In our increasingly flexible and thoroughly deregulated job market all prospects of arresting the rot, let alone restoring the fast-vanishing framework of prospective planning, grow bleaker by the hour.
>
> (Bauman 2001: 132)

'Prospective planning' of learning, curriculum as prescription, is then colossally inappropriate to the flexible work order – on this analysis it is doomed and will require rapid replacement by new forms of learning organisation. Both authors have written about the significance of narrative in learning. 'The Learning Lives' project (2003–8), in which Goodson worked, developed a series of studies of narrative learning in action, and the book *Narrative Learning* pursues the argument for taking narrative seriously as a context for learning (Goodson and Biesta 2009). The context-based, object-driven inquiry approach to curriculum (Deakin Crick 2009) debated in this chapter presents significant theoretical and practical resources to address this need, because it takes seriously the 'self' who is learning, with his or her particular life story and aspirations, and moves progressively towards the construction of knowledge and the recognition and use of the forms of knowledge present in the 'prescribed curriculum', which still forms the material for mass public assessment and validation. In several studies of this methodology, the use of narrative has emerged as a crucial pedagogical tool as well as a pervasive culture (Millner *et al.* 2006; Deakin Crick 2006; Deakin Crick *et al.* 2007; Cole *et al.* 2007; Deakin Crick 2009). In the next section we explore some of the ways in which narrative operates within this approach to curriculum.

Curriculum as narration

Many of these young people were descendants of the 'stolen generation'; that is, their parents and grandparents were those Indigenous babies and children who were forcibly moved from their families during the twentieth century (as a means of cultural assimilation) and 'relocated' with white Australian families or in 'homes' many miles away. Although the Australian government has now formally apologised for this policy, and is seeking in every way to redress the balance, the legacy is one of broken stories, broken trust and social dislocation within these traditional communities. As White and Wyn argue:

> The fundamental backdrop to these experiences is colonialism and the terrible legacies of invasion and dispossession. The structural disadvantages generated in and through the colonial process are acknowledged as playing a major part in the lives and prospects of young Indigenous peoples today. Colonialism has shaped their past and their present. It continues to heavily influence the contours of their future.
>
> (White and Wyn 2008: 66)

These students are typically disengaged from formal Western-style schooling and, to a significant extent in this study, they are also disengaged from their traditional heritage. However, traditions and memories remain with many of the elders in these communities, who still provide a connection for these young people with their history and customs, and thus with their Indigenous identity.

The examples used in this chapter are all drawn from a group of adolescent Indigenous students in the 'Learning Place and Identity' project, who embarked with their teachers and mentors on personalised, inquiry-based learning journeys during 2008. These young people are the next generation of Indigenous people of this community, who have been dislocated from their culture. Fear of having children removed and other oppressive acts were what made their cultural practices go underground. However, these were not completely lost – the elders still provide the connection for these young people to claim back the knowledge that is rightfully theirs.

The project was a researcher-manipulated evaluation, in which the intervention was the inquiry-based learning project methodology discussed by Deakin Crick (2009). The students were invited to participate in a withdrawal project, based in the Ka Wul Centre: a learning centre on the school premises, which is dedicated to the Indigenous community. Students chose their teachers as mentors for their 'learning journey', which was implemented over three school terms.

Students received, on average, one hour per week of supervision in their projects. Qualitative data collection was undertaken by an external researcher and included focus group interviews, interviews with students and teachers, analysis of documentation and over 50 hours of video evidence of key stages of the process. The data used in this example has been selected from the overall data set as an in-depth example how 'narrative' functioned in the students' learning journeys (the eight-step process).

In this programme, they were invited to participate in a personalised inquiry project, through selecting an artefact or a place that was personally significant to them. Over the holidays they took a digital camera home and took 24 pictures of places, or objects, that were important to them. These images then formed a bank of possibilities for the starting point of their inquiry. The idea was for the young people to be able to describe why and how this object or place was important to them, and how it fitted into their life story. In order to engage authentically with the process, the teachers also selected some artefacts for discussion. This process was profound for both students and teachers because it gave them a deeper glimpse of the 'other' as a whole person, and some sense of their life story. One teacher described how important it was to connect with the student as a whole person in this way:

> I think it was quite good from both points of view. [A] seemed to relax a bit more around me. She's a student that I know because I teach her for science so I see one side of her there and she sees one side of me and this was a chance for us to talk about things outside of school and I actually picked up quite a lot about [A] from her objects.
>
> (Interview with teacher from the Learning
> Place and Identity project)

A student describes the object he chose and why he selected it:

Student: Yeah, I had to pick my top thing and then do one of those things about it.
Researcher: So we picked...?
Student: My dog Toby.
Researcher: I notice he's got a lovely heart around him... tell me why you picked him?
Student: Well because I got him from my mum's cousin and I haven't saw her for a long time, yeah and yeah, that's probably it.
Researcher: So what's special about Toby?
Student: We've had him for a bit over three years and yeah, I just like him I guess.
Researcher: So has sharing the objects and talking to your [teacher] helped you understand yourself as a learner?
Student: Yep.
Researcher: So what do you think has been the most important lesson there?

Student: How much I like Toby.
Researcher: What makes Toby special?
Student: He's the only dog that, when he runs away, he comes back.
[LAUGH]
Researcher: Oh well I'll tell you, most of them run away don't they?
Student: Yeah, because all my other dogs run away and then they don't come back.

> (Interview with student from the Learning
> Place and Identity project)

Another student, 'K', described what he discovered about his teacher:

> Yes well we did like this cover sheet thing ... it has like what are some of the special things you have learnt about your mentor and I wrote down like because he had like this photo of his family and I put that he loves his family. And then he had this rock which he dug up from underneath his house and I put that he likes adventures and that. And he had a picture ... a feather of a lyrebird and he told me the story about it. How he went in the bush and he heard these birds and that and it was the same bird, it was the lyrebird.

> (Interview with student from the Learning
> Place and Identity project)

Alongside this choosing activity, the students developed their own language for learning by identifying seven native Australian animals which would represent the personal qualities they need for learning how to learn, based on the seven dimensions of learning power (Deakin Crick *et al.* 2004; Cole *et al.*). For strategic awareness, for example, they chose the wedge-tailed eagle because it is able to fly at an altitude and circle on the air currents, whilst being able to see what is going on below. Already, this shared narrative formulation of the eagle's learning behaviour was forming an important part of the process. They identified particular qualities in the bird, which is a powerful traditional symbol, and projected onto the eagle some key learning qualities – such as the ability to see the big picture and to identify strategic possibilities. The students all had experiential knowledge of wedge-tailed eagles in the bush and presentational knowledge of the symbols and images that are traditionally used to represent them. The stories of the eagle (and the six other native animals) formed a basis for dialogue and the co-construction of new possibilities for being and identity. Because the images and metaphors for learning were closely aligned with traditional Indigenous images, symbols and rituals – and indeed their selection was undertaken in a relational, consensual manner in keeping with Indigenous decision making – the students were able to identify with these qualities in a deep way, which strengthened their own identities as Indigenous learners.

Developing narratives about the animals extended the students' understanding about taking responsibility for themselves as learners, utilising the power of metaphor to carry rich meanings and to bridge between three life worlds – their own life worlds, their traditional Indigenous culture and worldview, and the life world of learning in a Western-style school.

The shared and mentored construction of a bigger story, by the students themselves, led to a powerful, if unexpected, outcome. The story they wrote began with the seven animals being locked up in Taronga Zoo in Sydney – the eagle (strategic awareness), the echidna (resilience), Willy wagtail (creativity), the platypus (meaning making), the snake (changing and learning), the emu (critical curiosity) and the ants (learning relationships). The story began with their longing to escape:

> All the animals at Taronga thought about escaping from time to time. The same idea would come to each of them sooner or later: 'The trouble is, I'm just not getting anywhere, stuck in here! I'd really like to make something of my life, do something different, see something different, experience something different … learn something new … return to my country where I could make a difference.'
>
> (Student narrative from the Learning Place and Identity project)

Each of the animals in the story modelled their own particular learning dispositions and as they began to talk with each other and share ideas, they began to realise they could make changes:

> For the first time since Willy Wagtail told him about his dreams, Snake felt a stirring of excitement wriggle all the way down his coils. He was beginning to get it. He started to feel himself grow and change. He was already learning to ask questions and be curious, like Emu. Now he was learning how important it is to be patient and stick at things, like Echidna. His skin felt tight, all of a sudden.
>
> (Ibid.)

The animals carefully constructed a way of working together and a strategy that would enable them to escape and find a new life. The eagle played a key role in the story, drawing together all animals into a team:

> A shape flashed across the light of the moon and its shadow fell momentarily on the scene. All the animals fell silent. The Eagle landed, a little higher up the leaning gum tree, spread her wings magnificently and folded them away with a shake of her feathers. No one spoke. They were all curious to hear what the Eagle was going to say.
>
> 'The moment has arrived. We have anticipated it. Now, everything is in place. Under the full moon, I have called you together to combine your strengths, summon the power of all your learning and fulfil your dream. I have planned for this night. I see everything, from the smallest ant to the whole zoo, the city and the vast bush, stretching out west as far as the eye

can see. I see each moment: how it arrived on the wings of the past and how it will launch into the great sky of the future. Learn from me as you have learned from each other. I give you your purpose, your direction, your focus and, most important of all, your readiness to accept your responsibility to yourself to achieve your dream,'

All the animals breathed a deep breath of the midnight air and solemnly vowed to accept their responsibility to themselves and the group. They knew that, before the night was over, if they all played their part, they would be free.

(Ibid.)

They go on to escape from the zoo, pursued by the zookeepers, and eventually find their way into the bush, near their school:

No one really knows how long the animals took to make it back to Wonnaruah country but when they arrived they began to get busy and learnt how to live out their dreams, by following the knowledge that was there waiting for them, as old as the land itself. They understood that to achieve your goals you must become strong in your culture and bring it into your learning so that you can make sense of the path to success. They understood that they must encourage one another to be successful and live out new dreams.

One day, they got together again and agreed that they should leave the bush. One dream had been fulfilled. The city children had been sad to lose them. The bush would always be there when they needed to go back to it. They had learned how to travel. They had all survived crossing the F3, the busiest road in their world, to get back to the country. It had taken skill, determination and courage to do it but together they had made it, and had learnt together how to do it.

Now, they knew they would go on learning for the rest of their lives. They would never go back to the zoo. They had returned home to the Hunter Valley, home to the Wonnaruah people, their home. Today the animals are working around the schools of the Singleton area, helping children and students to grow and change by passing on their truths and being everlasting symbols of what they discovered on their adventure.

On a winter's night, in the light of a full moon, a silver snake skin lay glistening on the ground, near a billabong beside a fallen gum tree. The wind gets up and whistles and snaps through the telegraph wires, singing a brave note in Wonnarua language, which seems to be saying, 'Follow your dreams, buddy! Follow your dreams ... dreams ... dreams'.

(Ibid.)

The shared construction of this story by the students themselves, the mentoring processes around literacy, the approval of the community elders of the final version and its publication, all formed a crucial part of the process of inquiry for these youngsters. They were deeply engaged with their own learning and motivated to become knowledge workers – making knowledge and skills work for them in the co-creation of meaningful, new knowledge. The 'spin-offs', in terms of cognitive outcomes and engagement, were significant. Their individual life stories connected with the shared story, which itself connected with the bigger political and cultural stories of their tradition.

In their personalised learning projects these students embarked on the eight-step process (Deakin Crick 2009), drawing on their personal and newly constructed traditional stories to move from their chosen artefact towards the construction of new knowledge. The process of co-construction of knowledge was facilitated not only through the explicit use of the learning dispositions as tools – for example, using my critical curiosity to generate questions – but through 'storying'. That is, through moving from meaningful questions to uncovering the narratives embedded in the object or place of their inquiry.

'K' eventually chose his grandfather's pocket watch as the starting point for his inquiry. He discovered when it was made and by whom, and that it was called 'antique'; that his father collects antique objects; and that Victorian objects were made differently to new ones. These stories invited new questions, which led to new stories. Eventually he identified a key concept he wanted to explore further – collections. At the time of writing, he is working on a final project, which answers the question 'Why do people collect things?'

Discussion

Narratives are lived and experienced as well as told: they can be uncovered, created, told and re-told. Narratives are concrete and open-ended: they require flexibility, fidelity and imagination. They are experiential and, in telling, they provide a way of describing and connecting alternative life worlds, of constructing systems of symbols and values, rules and regulations, and permissions and power structures. In the examples described here, the power of curriculum as narration was evident in several ways.

First, in relation to engagement, human beings construct meaning through narrative. Our sense of our self is embedded in the stories we tell and re-tell. When a person's life story is in focus and both the process and content of learning connects with their life story, then they will make meaning and engage. Without engagement there will be little learning, and without a sense of self there will be little engagement. In these examples the students and teachers were deeply engaged in the processes of learning through simply listening to, and honouring, each other's stories. As the teachers commented, there is little space for this in a traditional curriculum.

Second, in relation to personal change, we change ourselves by changing the stories we tell about ourselves. We use stories in making sense of our experience and in the construction of meaning and purpose for our lives. Stories give us a reason for action and enable us to re-construct identity. Personal change is crucial to deep learning – indeed, some would argue that it is synonymous with it – and 're-storying' is crucial to personal change. By telling the story of his becoming like the wedge-tailed eagle, 'K' is engaging actively in the process of change. He is re-imagining his future.

Third, in relation to community and interaction, both individuals and communities construct stories as a primary means of understanding and negotiating their lives. These stories are built on an underlying structure of beliefs and commitments and can be both used and abused in building community identity. Stories operate within learning communities – and in our study, both teachers and students were re-constructing their stories in relation to what it means to be a teacher and what it means to be a learner, as well as re-constructing and narrating their shared story.

Fourth, in relation to cultural diversity and freedom, the data used in this example is drawn from an Indigenous community, for whom story, experience and relationships are profoundly important. Young people in these traditions are well sensitised to the power of story in many modes and to alternative ways of knowing. By accessing their traditional stories and crafting a new one in the context of schooling, they were doing several things. They were being political – thankfully in a context where that is now welcomed – because their story was about enslavement and empowerment. They were re-crafting an old story in a new context and continuing their own tradition – re-appropriating their cultural heritage. They were celebrating their shared sense of identity within a particular tradition.

It would be a mistake, however, to think that this is only relevant to Indigenous communities. All cultures and traditions have big stories – not all of them get told and not all of them are necessarily helpful. Culturally deprived and marginalised communities are fundamentally deprived of rich stories and of the sense of identity that comes with them. Western young people have grown up with the stories of Western progress and capitalism, with its individualism and scientific materialism as well as its stories of democracy and social justice. Those youngsters for whom this story 'sucks' (usually because they feel disenfranchised in some way) search for alternative stories and ways of belonging. These bigger stories carry the shared values and rules and regulations that shape what is possible or not possible in Western learning communities and, especially in times of profound change, require examination, re-telling and re-visioning.

Fifth, in relation to active citizenship, the discernment of story is a key to illuminating citizenship issues in learning. Drawing out and understanding the story elements in the construction of knowledge gives a broad perspective on the processes by which different societies have negotiated 'truth and right', and why people behave as they do in relation to the social and natural world. Communities gather stories about themselves and construct overarching stories about their community, which are sometimes buttressed by religious accounts of life. These become part of the very identity of the community and are points of reference in discussions about morality and political decision making. Yet stories upholding community identity frequently do so in part by stigmatising and alienating other people and other stories. A key factor in reconciliation is the ability to hear the story of the 'other'. In the example we have used, the students negotiated issues about the subjugation of one group by another – and, in the process, explored for themselves one of the most significant citizenship issues in Australian culture.

The negotiation of conflicting stories is one key characteristic of public conversation. To hear the voice of the 'other' is potentially to be enlarged in vision and understanding and thereby enable the community to make better decisions. The quality of public conversation is a crucial determinant of the health of a society.

Sixth, in relation to the co-construction of knowledge in the information age, as we argue elsewhere in this chapter, the pedagogical challenge is to bring curriculum provision closer to the material condition of humanity today (Jaros 2003). The top-down theorising that dominates the scientific method, as well as religious and philosophical systems of thought, must be regarded as just one of several objectives in curriculum provision. This personalised approach to inquiry-based learning is grounded in a local, context-based, bottom-up (genealogical) approach, which leads the learner from a direct, personal encounter with a place to the models of the world that constitute the core of traditional instruction and assessment (Jaros 2003; Jaros and Deakin Crick 2007). Uncovering the stories that shape or explain the place or context under investigation is a crucial step, which moves the learner beyond mere description and into the higher-order thinking and learning capabilities relating to problem formulation, the identification of key (abstract) concepts and knowledge mapping. This enables the learner to draw on the bigger models of the world (often explained through narrative, and situated within traditional disciplines), which are relevant for their analysis and problem solving.

Conclusions

There is currently a considerable amount of momentum in government circles for the advocacy of personalised learning and pupil voice. The relevance of narrative learning in this field is clear and highly adjacent. Moreover, life learning itself has become a major focus of policy makers – nationally and internationally. As it stands the agenda is very narrow, mainly focusing on the economic function of lifelong learning and on learning skills.

What we show is that learning – more specifically learning from life – goes on in the lives of people, is significant for them and is one of the main vehicles of education, for it is narrative; it involves constructing and telling stories about oneself and one's life. In this regard, we not only present a new way to understand learning but, through this, we are able to identify learning processes that are highly significant for individuals and therefore for society.

Our work seeks to define a new learning theory that, instead of dealing with learning as the learning of prescribed content (i.e. defined curriculum), explores learning that is involved in the construction of the ongoing maintenance of the life-story narrative. Evidence is presented that most people spend a good deal of time rehearsing and recounting their life story and it is a highly significant part of theory actions and agency. Hence, it is a very important site of learning in itself, with very substantial implications for the subsequent actions of the people involved. Moreover, since the people themselves are engaged in the construction of the narrative, there is not the normal problem that externally prescribed

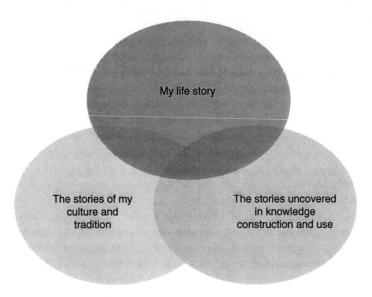

Figure 4.1 The dynamic interaction of three stories

curriculum has, of trying to ensure personal engagement. In so much of pre-scribed learning, for example, many students are quite clearly disengaged and disaffected and so, whatever the curriculum, it is of little relevance since there is no engagement. Narrative learning seeks to shift the focus to an area where, from the beginning, engagement and motivation are in place.

The dynamic interaction of three stories is at the heart of curriculum as nar-ration (see Figure 4.1).

When all three stories are available for telling and for dialogue, then narrative learning is possible. This also grounds the notion of 'personalisation', because it values and attends to the life story of the person who is learning as a core element of pedagogy, rather than an 'add-on', necessary for the disaffected students, but dispensable for those who succeed in the 'curriculum as prescription' model.

In this chapter we have explored the ways in which these three types of narra-tive operate in both the process and the content of inquiry-based learning. They require an open-ended, facilitative pedagogy in which power relations between learner and teacher change from that of expert–novice to facilitator–learning agent. The process is formative, and builds from the life narrative of the learner. The curriculum becomes a 'narratable pathway' towards the formation of iden-tity and agency when 'knowing as storying' is valued, promoted and represented. Narratives provide and create space for 'pedagogic moments' in which people can connect with themselves, each other, their own culture and tradition, their hopes and aspirations and ultimately with an intentional, mentored construction of knowledge, which serves their personal and public trajectories. This kind of narrative learning will provide an antidote to the prescriptive learning of curriculum that has disengaged generations of learners.

References

Bauman, Z. (2001) *The Individualized Society*, Cambridge: Polity Cambridge Press.

Bourdieu, P. and Passeron, J.C. (2000) *Reproduction in Education, Society and Culture* 2nd edition, London: Sage.

Cole, A., Small, T. and Deakin Crick, R. (2007) 'Getting started: learning power and young people not in education, employment or training', Bristol: ViTaL Partnerships Ltd.

Deakin Crick, R. (2006) 'Locked-up learning: learning power and young offenders', Bristol: ViTaL Partnerships Ltd.

Deakin Crick, R. (2007) 'Learning how to learn: the dynamic assessment of learning power', *Curriculum Journal*, 18(2), 135–53.

Deakin Crick, R. (2009) 'Inquiry-based learning: reconciling the personal and the public in a democratic and archaeological pedagogy', *Curriculum Journal*, 20, 1.

Deakin Crick, R., Broadfoot, P. and Claxton, G. (2004) 'Developing an effective lifelong learning inventory: the Elli Project', *Assessment in Education*, 11 (3), 248–72.

Deakin Crick, R., Small, T., Jaros, M., Pollard, K., Leo, E., Hearne, P., James, L. and Milner, N. (2007) 'Inquiring minds: transforming potential through personalised learning', London: RSA.

Goodson, I.F. (1993) *School Subjects and Curriculum Change*, 3rd edition, London: Falmer Press.

Goodson, I.F. (1995) *The Making of Curriculum*, London: Falmer Press.

Goodson, I.F. (2005) *Learning Curriculum, and Life Politics*, London: Routledge.

Goodson, I.F. and Biesta, G. (2009) *Narrative Learning*, London and New York: Routledge.

Jaros, M. (2003) 'Onto-poetic applications of mathematical analogy in arts and literature', *Consciousness, Literature and the Arts*, 4 (2).

Jaros, M. and Deakin Crick, R. (2007) 'Personalised learning in the post mechanical age', *Journal of Curriculum Studies*, 39(4), 423–40.

Layton, D. (1973) *Science for the People*, London: George Allen and Unwin.

Learning Lives (2003–2008) 'Learning lives: learning, identity and agency in the life course', ESRC Teaching and Learning Research Programme, with G. Biesta and F. Macleod, University of Exeter; J. Field, University of Stirling; P. Hodkinson, University of Leeds. Available at: www.tlrp.org/proj/phase111/biesta.htm (accessed 6 August 2013).

Mead, M. (1964) *Continuity in Cultural Evolution*, New Haven: Yale University Press.

Millner, N., Small, T. and Deakin Crick, R. (2006) 'Learning by accident', Bristol: ViTaL Partnerships.

White, R. and Wyn, J. (2008) *Youth and Society, Exploring the Social Dynamic of Youth Experience*, Oxford: Oxford University Press.

Part II

5 The rise of the life narrative

> When we go on about the big things, the political situation, global warming, world poverty, it all looks really terrible, with nothing getting better, nothing to look forward to. But when I think small, closer in – you – know a girl I've just met, or this song we're going to do with Chas, or snowboarding next month, then it looks great. So this is going to be my motto-think small.
>
> (McEwan 2005: 34–5)

There is a kind of popular consensus at the moment that we live in 'an age of narrative'. The truth is rather more complex, for although it is true that narratives and stories are part of the common currency of the day, the scale of those narratives, their scope and aspiration, has dramatically changed. In fact we are entering a period of particular kinds of narratives: life narratives and small-scale narratives.

In past periods there have been 'grand narratives' of human intention and progress. Hywell Williams, in his recent chronological history of the world, argues that the link between human history and progress in grand narrative grew exponentially in the mid-nineteenth century. He says that the progress narratives that emerged at this time were often 'brash and naïve':

> It was certainly founded on the fact of material advance – the sudden and greater ease of travel, improvements in sanitation and the reduction in disease, which so impressed contemporaries in the advanced West. These victories also seemed to signify a real moral progress.
>
> Nobody supposed that humanity was getting better at producing saints and geniuses but there was a new confidence in the possibility of a well-ordered society. The intellectual advances that were once the preserve of an educated elite had spread further.
>
> (Williams 2005: 18)

Commenting on the public life associated with these changes, he says:

> Once, the sceptical courtiers of the eighteenth century had sneered at superstition in gossipy little groups – a century later greater masses of people

debated great issues of religion and science, political reform and freedom of trade in public meetings.

(Ibid.)

In the last sentence we can see how far public engagement has fallen – the idea of great masses of people debating great issues is inconceivable in the present world. In part, this is closely related to the decline of narrative scope and aspiration.

In the twentieth century, we have witnessed the collapse of grand narratives. Again Williams provides a valuable summary:

> The idea of the grand narrative in the human sciences has fallen out of fashion. Christian providence, Freudian psychology, positivist sciences, Marxist class consciousness, nationalist autonomy, fascist will: all have attempted to supply narratives that shape the past. When it comes to practical politics, some of these narratives proved to involve repression and death.
>
> The history of the twentieth century dissolved the connection between material and scientific progress and a better moral order. Technological advance was twice turned to the business of mass slaughter in global war, as well as genocide and ethnic cleansing. Material progress was seen to mingle with moral regress. The Model T Ford and the gas chamber were the inventions that defined the century.
>
> (Williams 2005: 18)

We can then begin to see how grand narratives fell from grace, losing not only scope and aspiration but also our underpinning faith in their general capacity to guide or shape our destiny. From the vortex left after the collapse of the grand narratives, we see the emergence of another kind of narrative, infinitely smaller in scope, often individualised – the personal life story. It reflects a dramatic change in the scale of human belief and aspiration. Alongside these small narratives we also see a return to older, more fundamentalist precepts.

How has this transformation of the role and scope of narrative been worked? How is the new genre socially constructed? Writing in 1996, I argued that literature and art are normally ahead of other cultural carriers of ideology in providing us with new scripts, and defining our personal narratives and 'life politics'. I said we should locate 'our scrutiny of stories to show that the general forms, skeletons and ideologies that we employ in structuring the way we tell our individual tales come from a wider culture' (Goodson 2005: 215).

Following this scrutiny, I think we can see in contemporary cultural activity how the move to smaller, more individual life narratives is emerging. Interestingly, this is often referred to as the 'age of narrative': of narrative politics, of narrative storytelling, of narrative identity. Put in historical perspective against the last centuries following the Age of Enlightenment, we should see this as the beginning, not of the 'age of narratives', but of the 'age of small narratives'. In our current individualised society, our art, culture and politics increasingly reflect a move to highly individualised or special-interest narratives, which often draw on the literature of therapy and personal and self-development.

Perhaps a few examples from the work of some of our cultural icons will illustrate the point. Bruce Springsteen, the American rock star, has I think always been one of the best and most perceptive storytellers. He writes his songs very carefully and works on quite large canvases of human aspiration at times, such as his album *The River*. In this album he reflects, in line with Bob Dylan, who recently wrote that he 'hadn't got a dream that hadn't been repossessed', on the limiting of human dreams. Springsteen wrote, 'Is a dream a lie if it don't come true, or is it something worse?' These reflections on the capacity of larger human aspirations to direct our life narratives have recently driven him in a more specific, individual direction. His album *The Ghost of Tom Joad* profoundly reflects in its title, as well as in its substance, an awareness of a massive shift in narrative scope. Tom Joad, of course, the figure in Steinbeck's *Grapes of Wrath* (1939), carries a storyline linked to mass movements, which aimed to provide social justice at a time of global business depression. Once this link between individual storylines and collective aspirations is broken, we enter the epoch of small narratives, the world of individualised 'life politics'.

In a sense, Springsteen's latest work, such as *Devils and Dust*, reflects the move we are describing: the move from grand narratives linked to political engagement, towards individual life narratives and, more specifically, focused on life politics. We can see how this seismic shift in narrative capacity is explored and scripted in the work of our creative artists. Returning to the focus of Springsteen's *The Ghost of Tom Joad*, we see a retrospective look at narrative linked to social and political purpose; but his new album moves off into an individual life-narrative focus. Sean O'Hagan writes that: 'Unlike *The Ghost of Tom Joad* it possesses none of that album's pointed social awareness. Instead we get a set of intimate and often fragmentary glimpses of ordinary people's lives in trouble' (O'Hagan 2005: 7). 'What I have done on this record,' elaborates Springsteen on the DVD, 'is to write specific narrative stories about people whose souls are in danger or are at risk from where they are in the world or what the world is bringing to them' (ibid.).

Once again, then, Springsteen tries to link his narratives to a broader tradition, but this time the link is largely rhetorical, for the stories now are fragmentary and individualised, and without reference to broader social movements (beyond the nebulous 'folk tradition'). As he says, he now writes 'specific narrative stories' about people and the passivity of the response is reflected in his phrase that these people are 'at risk from where they are in the world or what the world is bringing to them'. The scope and aspiration of narratives is finely elaborated in this quote, and it illustrates the seismic shift in the narrative capacity that has happened over the past two centuries.

The same redefinition of narrative capacity can be seen in film-making. Many film-makers articulate their use of specific life narratives in contemporary film-making. Jorge Semprun, for example, who has made some of the most resonant political films, said recently in an interview that:

the atmosphere in May '68 and its aftermath created an appetite for political films ... But today the mood is different. If you are to make a political film

now you have to approach it not from the point of a nation or national struggle, but one of individual choice.

(Semprun 2004: 4)

Gil Troy, a history professor writing in *The New York Times*, put it the same way
when contemplating the possibilities of action in the contemporary world: 'Our
challenge today is to find meaning not in a national crisis, but in an individual's
daily life' (Troy 1999: A27).

Reviewing new books on Derrida and Marx, Dolon Cummings recently
reflected on these changes in the reach of theoretical narrative in looking at the
differences between the two writers:

> For theory to 'grip the masses,' as Marx puts it, there has to be at least the
> foundation of a mass movement for it to address. Without such a movement,
> theory lacks direction, discipline even. Consequently the obscurity of con-
> temporary philosophy as exemplified by Derrida and his followers is not a
> purely intellectual phenomenon. Disconnected from political engagement
> reading lacks urgency and how we read and what becomes almost arbitrary.
>
> (Cummings 2006: 39)

Cummings adds a very significant last sentence: 'But the question of how to read
any author cannot be entirely separated from the question of how to live, and
that is a question that never really goes away' (ibid.: 39).

We see here the changing canvas for narrative construction and the dramatic
change in scope and aspiration, and we can see this reflected in our social and
political life. The change can be seen in the political adviser on network TV who
recently put it this way, which I have paraphrased: 'No it's not that we see the
need to change the policy in response to public opposition ... no, not at all ... our
conclusion is that we need to change the story we tell about the policy.'

This is a perfect redefinition of the new genre of 'narrative politics'. New in
one sense, but in fact it dates back some way in time – most significantly to the
public relations guru, Edward Bernays. Bernays believed we could manipulate
people's unconscious desires and, by appealing to them, we could sell anything –
from soap powder to political policies. It was a matter of crafting the right kind
of story. Hence:

> You didn't vote for a political party out of duty, or because you believed it
> had the best policies to advance the common good; you did so because of a
> secret feeling that it offered you the most likely opportunity to promote
> yourself.
>
> (Adams 2002: 5)

As Christopher Cauldwell has noted, as a result of the triumph of narrative politics: 'Politics has gone from largely being about capital and labour to being

largely about identity and sovereignty' (Cauldwell 2005). Politicians appear to understand this need for narrative fine-tuning as they hone their policies. The narrative matters more than the substance, as this quote from the late lamented Charles Kennedy makes clear: 'Whilst we had good and quite popular policies [pause] we have got to find and fashion a narrative' (quoted in Branigan 2005: 8).

In previous generations, his Old Etonian and Oxford connections would have provided an authoritative narrative through which to promote his political ambitions. The cultural and symbolic capital of such an education would then have come with an implicit and very powerful storyline. These places traditionally produced those who govern us, whilst the symbolic and social capital that they engender are still largely intact. Cameron has predictably worried about constructing an acceptable life narrative.

The dilemma is outlined in this interview with Martin Bentham (2005), undertaken before Cameron became leader:

> But as Cameron insists, it is not just his preference for racy television programmes that calls into question the stereotyped image that others have placed upon him. He cites his liking for the 'gloomy left-wing' music of bands such as the Smiths, Radiohead, and Snow Patrol, which brings ribbing from his friends, as a further example of his divergence from the traditional Tory image, and also, perhaps rather rashly for a newly appointed shadow Education Secretary, admits to regularly misbehaving 'in all sorts of ways' while at school.
>
> Most importantly, however, he says that what keeps him connected very firmly in ordinary life is the job of representing his constituents in Witney, Oxfordshire, and life at home with his wife, Samantha, and their two children, three-year-old Ivan, who suffers from cerebral palsy and epilepsy, and Nancy, who is aged 14 months.
>
> 'Am I too posh to push?' he quips, before determinedly explaining why he rejects the criticism of his background. 'In the sort of politics I believe in it shouldn't matter what you've had in the past, it's what you are going to contribute in the future, and I think that should be true of everybody, from all parts of society, all colours and ages and races, and I hope that goes for Old Etonians too.'
>
> (Bentham 2005: 10)

What I think Cameron has noted is that if he re-crafts his life narrative 'it shouldn't matter what you've had in the past'. In other words, he is worried that his life experience of sustained systematic privilege will interfere with the narrative he is trying to create for himself and his party, where there is a 'genuine care and compassion for those who fall behind' and where what 'people really want (is) a practical down-to-earth alternative to Labour'. He ends, 'Am I too posh? It shouldn't really matter where you come from – even if it's Eton.' Whilst Eton may have massive historical claims to cultural and symbolic capital, the narrative capital it provides is clearly a little more difficult to present and cash in on. Cameron's honest appraisal of the dilemma elegantly illustrates the seismic shift towards narrative politics and how this is likely to feed through into new educational modes for acquiring narrative capital (see Goodson 2004).

The same importance of narrative capital can be seen working its way into the literature on business management and leadership. Peter Senge's (1990) work on the discipline of business leaders points to the salience of what he calls the 'principal story' in the motivation and direction of business leaders.

To forge a link between the multinational and the personal, we need to grasp each person's life theme. Senge says this about purpose stories:

> The interviews that I conducted as background for this chapter led to what was, for me, a surprising discovery. Although the three leaders with whom I talked operate in completely different industries – a traditional service business, a traditional manufacturing business, and a high-tech manufacturing business – and although the specifics of their views differed substantially, they each appeared to draw their own inspiration from the same source. Each perceived a deep story and a sense of purpose that lay behind his vision, what we have come to call the purpose story – a larger pattern of becoming that gives meaning to his personal aspirations and his hopes for their organization. For O'Brien the story has to do with 'the ascent of man.' For Simon, it has to do with 'living in a more creative orientation'. For Ray Stat, it has to do 'with integrating thinking and doing'.
>
> This realization came late one evening, after a very long day with the tape and transcript of one of the interviews. I began to see that these leaders were doing something different from just 'storytelling,' in the sense of using stories to teach lessons or transmit bits of wisdom. They were relating the story – the overarching explanation of why they do what they do, how their organizations need to evolve, and how this evolution is part of something larger. As I reflected back on gifted leaders whom I have known, I realised that this 'larger story' was common to them all, and conversely that many otherwise competent managers in leadership positions were not leaders of the same ilk precisely because they saw no larger story.
>
> The leader's purpose story is both personal and universal. It defines her or his life's work. It ennobles his efforts, yet leaves an abiding humility that keeps him from taking his own successes and failures too seriously. It brings a unique depth to meaning to his vision, a larger landscape upon which his personal dreams and goals stand out as landmarks on a longer journey. But what is important, this story is central to his ability to lead. It places his organization's purpose, its reason for being within a context of 'where we've come from and where we're headed,' where the 'we' goes beyond the organization itself to humankind more broadly. In this sense, they naturally see their organization as a vehicle for bringing learning and

change into society. This is the power of the purpose story – it provides a single integrating set of ideas that give meaning to all aspects of a leader's work.

(Senge 1990: 346)

The pattern of narrative construction can now be discerned at work in the advertising industry. In previous times advertising was a mass movement, which meant it targeted large segments of the population and addressed them through the mass media of television, radio and the press. Whilst this was not a process free of narrative construction, and was indeed deeply impregnated in this way, it was the narrative construction of collective identities and collective desires that could be reached through the mass media. These were not grand narratives, but they were certainly large narratives aimed at significant sections of the population. This collective narrative advertising is beginning to break down in the face of the rise of the small narrative and the individualised society. The evidence is everywhere. To give one piece of evidence: in the last year, advertising revenues were down 3.5 per cent for the national press, 4.5 per cent for commercial radio and 3.3 per cent for one of the main commercial television stations (ITV1). These are very significant reductions over a one-year period, and they indicate the beginning of a sharp decline in mass narrative advertising. In its place, according to the National Consumer Council, is a wholly different pattern of advertising. In contrast to the figures above, advertising on the Internet rose by 70 per cent last year. This is a seismic shift in the size and aspiration of advertising. A spokesman for the National Consumer Council said:

> The point about the Internet is that people can be told individually tailored stories which fit their own prejudices and predilections. The advertiser can access all this niche information and can tailor individual and personalised narratives for each individual taste. This is likely to be much more successful than the hit-and-miss mass advertising of the past.
>
> (Interview on *BBC News*, 23 March 2006)

We can see then how the 'age of small narratives', of life narratives, has been expressed in emerging patterns of art, politics and business. In this sense the problematics of studying people's lives are part of a wider context of social relations, proprieties and provisions. Lasch, for instance, has scrutinised the historical trajectory of private lives in *Haven in a Heartless World* (Lasch 1977). In his history of modern society, he discerns two distinct phases. In the first phase, he argues that the division of labour that accompanied the development of individual capitalism deprived ordinary people of control over their work, making that work alienating and unfulfilling. In the second phase, Lasch argues that liberalism promoted a view that, whilst work might be alienated under capitalism, all could be restored in the private domain. 'It was agreed that people would be freed to pursue happiness and virtue in their private lives in whatever manner they chose.' The workplace was this severed form; the home and the family became the 'haven in the heartless world' (Menaud 1991). No sooner was this equation established, Lasch argues, than liberalism reneged:

> Private life was opening up to the 'helping' professions: doctors, teachers, psychologists, child guidance experts, juvenile court officers, and the like. The private domain was immediately made prey to these quasi-official 'forces of organised virtue' and 'the hope that private transactions could make up for the collapse of communal traditions and civic order' was smothered by the helping professions.
>
> (Lasch 1977: 168)

Interestingly, Denzin has recently argued that ethnographers and biographers represent the latest wave in this 'penetration' of private lives, and that this is to be expected at a time when we see 'the emergence of a new conservative politics of health and morality, centering on sexuality, the family and the individual' (Denzin 1991: 2).
  Hence he argues:

> The biography and the autobiography are among Reagan's legacy to American society. In these writing forms the liberal and left American academic scholarly community reasserts a commitment to the value of individual lives and their accurate representation in the life story document. The story thus becomes the left's answer to the repressive conservative politics of the last two decades of American history. With this method the sorrowful tales of America's underclass can be told. In such tellings a romantic and political identification with the downtrodden will be produced. From this identification will come a new politics of protest; a politics grounded in the harsh and raw economics, racial, and sexual edges of contemporary life. This method will reveal how large social groupings are unable to either live out their ideological versions of the American dream, or to experience personal happiness.
>
> (Ibid.)

And further:

> In re-inscribing the real life, with all its nuances, innuendoes and terrors, in the life story, researchers perpetuate a commitment to the production of realist, melodramatic, social problems texts which create an identification with the downtrodden in American society. These works of realism reproduce and mirror the social structures that need to be changed. They valorise the subjectivity of the powerless individual. They make a hero of the interactionist-ethnographer voyeur who comes back from the field with moving tales of the dispossessed. They work from an ideological bias that emphasises the situational, adjustive, and normative approach to social problems and their resolutions, whether this be in the classroom, the street, or the home.
>
> (Ibid.: 2–3)

The rise of the life narrative clearly comes with a range of problems, and also possibilities, for the social scientist. By scrutinising the wider social context of life narratives, we can begin to appreciate the dilemmas of qualitative work, which focuses on personal narratives and life stories.

The version of 'personal' that has been constructed and worked for in some Western countries is a particular version, an individualistic version, of being a person. It is unrecognisable to much of the rest of the world. But so many of the stories and narratives we have of teachers work unproblematically and without comment with this version of personal being and personal knowledge. Masking the limits of individualism, such accounts often present 'isolation, estrangement, and loneliness ... as autonomy, independence and self-reliance' (Andrews 1991: 13). Andrews concludes that if we ignore social context, we deprive ourselves, and our collaborators, of meaning and understanding. She says, 'It would seem apparent that the context in which human lives are lived is central to the core of meaning in those lives' and argues that 'researchers should not, therefore, feel at liberty to discuss or analyse how individuals perceive meaning in their lives and in the world around them, whilst ignoring the content and context of that meaning' (ibid.).

The truth is that, many times, a life storyteller will neglect the structural context of their lives or interpret such contextual forces from a biased point of view. As Denzin says, 'Many times a person will act as if he or she made his or her own history when, in fact, he or she was forced to make the history he or she lived' (Denzin 1989: 74). He gives an example from the 1986 study of alcoholics: 'You know I made the last four months, by myself. I haven't used or drank. I'm really proud of myself. I did it' (ibid.: 74–5). A friend, listening to this account, commented:

> You know you were under a court order all last year. You know you didn't do this on your own. You were forced to, whether you want to accept this fact or not. You also went to AA and NA. Listen Buster you did what you did because you had help and because you were afraid, and thought you had no other choice. Don't give me this 'I did it on my own' crap.
>
> (Ibid.)

The speaker replies, 'I know. I just don't like to admit it.' Denzin concludes:

> This listener invokes two structural forces, the state and AA, which accounted in part for this speaker's experience. To have secured only the speaker's account, without a knowledge of his biography and personal history, would have produced a biased interpretation of his situation.
>
> (Ibid.)

The story, then, provides a starting point for developing further understandings of the social construction of subjectivity; if the stories stay at the level of the personal and practical, we forego that opportunity. Speaking of the narrative method focusing on personal and practical teachers' knowledge, Willinsky writes: 'I am concerned that a research process [that] intends to recover the personal and

Subjectivity

experiential would pave over this construction site in its search for an overarching unity in the individual's narrative' (Willinsky 1989: 259).

These are the issues that begin to confront us as the age of the life narrative gathers pace. Let us therefore review some of the problems that we face when working with individual life narratives. First, the personal life story is an *individualising* device if divorced from context. It focuses on the uniqueness of individual personality and circumstance and in doing so may well obscure or ignore collective circumstances and historical movements. Life stories are only constructed in a specific historical circumstance and cultural conditions – these have to be bought into our methodological grasp.

Second, the individual life story, far from being personally constructed, is itself 'scripted'. The social scripts that people employ in telling their life stories are derived from a small number of archetypes available in the wider society. The life story script, far from being autonomous, is highly dependent on wider social scripts. In a sense, what we get when we listen to a life story is a combination of archetypal stories derived from wider social forces and the personal characterisations invoked by the life storyteller. The life story, therefore, has to be culturally located as we pursue our understandings.

In general, life stories themselves do not acknowledge this cultural location explicitly; neither do they reflect explicitly on their historical location in a particular time and place. The life story as data, therefore, faces a third dilemma in that it can be a 'de-contextualising' device, or at the very least an under-contextualising device. This means that the historical context of life stories needs to be further elucidated and they need to be understood in relationship to time and periodisation. We can think of time, as the French Annalistes do, as existing at a number of levels.

First, there is broad historical time – the large sweeps and periods of human history – what the Annalistes called the *longue durée*. Then there is generational or cohort time – the specific experiences of particular generations, say the 'baby boomers' born after the Second World War. Then there is cyclical time – the stages of the life cycle from birth through to work and childrearing (for some) through to retirement and death. Finally, there is personal time – the way each person develops phases and patterns according to personal dreams, objectives or imperatives across the life course.

These historical factors associated with time and period have to be addressed as we develop our understandings of life story data. This scrutiny of historical context, more broadly conceived, will also allow us to interrogate the issue of individualising and scripting mentioned earlier. The aim is to provide a story of individual action within a theory of context. This aim is served when we make the transition from life story studies to life histories.

Learning Lives: an example

The Learning Lives project took place between 2004 and 2008 and was funded by the Economic Social Research Council in Britain.

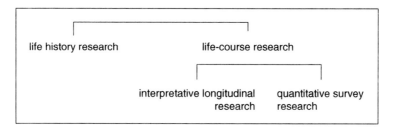

Figure 5.1 Learning Lives

From initial analysis of the texts, a number of broad themes have emerged. In this case the theme was around the importance placed on early childhood experiences to explain later life events and choices. The respondent whose stories we use in this chapter is one of the respondents who fit into this themed group. The stories have been selected to provide an overview of the range of experiences in childhood and adolescence that may be seen as important for identity formation in later life, and for the quests that have developed from these experiences.

What makes the project unusual is not only its length (a data-collection period of almost three years) and size (about 750 in-depth interviews with 150 adults aged 25 and older, plus a longitudinal questionnaire study with 1,200 participants), but also the fact that it combines two distinct research approaches: life history research and life-course research and that, within the latter approach, it utilises a combination of interpretative longitudinal research and quantitative survey research (see Figure 5.1).

In the Learning Lives project, we have the chance to see how life history can elucidate learning responses. What we do in the project is to deal with learning as one of the strategies people employ as the response to events in their lives. The great virtue of this situation, regarding our understanding of learning within the whole life context, is that we get some sense of the issue of engagement in learning as it relates to people living their lives. When we see learning as a response to actual events, then the issue of engagement can be taken for granted. So much of the literature on learning fails to address this crucial question of 'engagement' and, as a result, learning is seen as some formal task that is unrelated to the needs and interests of the learner. Hence so much of curriculum planning is based on prescriptive definitions of what is to be learnt without any understanding of the situation within the learners' lives. As a result, a vast amount of curriculum planning is abortive because the learner simply does not engage. To see learning as located within a life history is to understand that learning is contextually situated and that it also has a history, in terms of (1) the individual's life story, (2) the history and trajectories of the institutions that offer formal learning opportunities and (3) the histories of the communities and locations in which informal learning takes place. In terms of transitional spaces, we can see learning as a response to incidental transitions, such as events related to

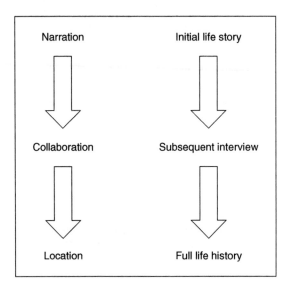

Figure 5.2 Developing life history interviews

illness, unemployment and domestic dysfunction, as well as the more structured transitions related to credentialing or retirement. Hence, these transitional events create encounters with formal, informal and primal learning opportunities.

How then do we organise our work to make sure that our collection of life narratives and learning narratives does not fall into the traps of individualisation, scripting and de-contextualisation? The answer is we try to build in an ongoing concern with time and historical period, and context and historical location. In studying learning, like any social practice, we need to build in an understanding of the context – historical and social – in which that learning takes place. This means that our initial collection of life stories, as narrated, moves on to become a collaboration with our life storytellers about the historical and social context of their lives. By the end, we hope the life story becomes the life history because it is located in historical time and context. Our sequence then moves as shown in Figure 5.2.

Let me give one concrete example of how location might work in studying teachers' lives. In the life stories of teachers, nowadays, the normal storyline is one of technicians who follow government guidelines and teach a curriculum that is prescribed by governments or departments of education. The storyline therefore reflects a particular historical moment where the teachers' work is constructed in a particular way. If, however, one compares current teacher storylines in England with the storylines collected 30 or 40 years ago, those stories would be of professionals who have autonomy and the capacity to decide what curriculum to teach and what content is organised to carry that curriculum. In seeking to locate the life story of current teachers, we would have to talk about the ongoing construction of the teachers' work in a particular way. In coming to understand how contemporary teachers' work provides a particular work context, we would get some sense of the historical context of teachers' work and how this is subject to change and transition as the historical circumstances of schooling change. Hence in moving from narration through to location, a historical understanding of the teachers' work might emerge.

So this is how time and context might emerge within life history research. To make sure that this temporal aspect is fully engaged within the project, we have divided our research between life history research and life-course research. In this way, the historical context of learning can be examined either retrospectively or in contemporary 'real time'. The retrospective understanding of the learning biography can be explored in life history research, whilst the real-time understanding of the ways in which learning biographies are lived can be understood through longitudinal life-course research. In this way, we set retrospective life history research against contemporary longitudinal life-course research.

We have summarised the rationale for combining these two approaches in this way:

> The reason for combining the two approaches is not only that it increases the time span available for investigation (albeit that the retrospective study of the learning biography can only be done through the accounts and recollections of participants).
>
> It is also because we believe that the combination of the two approaches allows us to see more and gain a better understanding than if we would only use one of them.
>
> To put it simply: life-history research can add depth to the interpretation of the outcomes of longitudinal life-course research, while life-course research can help to unravel the complexities of life-history research. Each, in other words, is a potential source for contextualizing and interpreting the findings of the other.
>
> (Biesta *et al.* 2004)

By moving from life stories towards full life histories, and by building in life-course analysis, we maximise the potential for understanding how time and context impinge on people's 'learning lives'. Such work, then, tries to put the individual life narrative back together with the collective context. In doing so, it seeks to heal the rupture between the individual life narrative and the collective and historical experience.

The next chapters explore how this might work in the study of teachers' professional knowledge and lives.

References

Adams, T. (2002) 'How Freud got under our skin', *Observer Review*, 10 March.

Andrews, M. (1991) *Lifetimes of Commitment: Ageing, Politics and Psychology*, London: Routledge.

Bentham, M. (2005) 'Tories' young pretender insists on a fair chance for all', *The Observer*, 15 May.

Biesta, G.J.J., Hodkinson, P. and Goodson, I.F. (2004) 'Combining life history and life-course approaches in researching lifelong learning: some methodological observations from the Learning Lives Project', paper presented at the annual Conference of Teaching and Learning Research Programme, 22–25 November.

Branigan, T, (2005) 'Kennedy prepares for the next step', *The Guardian*, 20 May.

Cauldwell, C. (2005) 'The final round for party politics', *The Financial Times*, 19–20 November.

Cummings, D. (2006) 'Thinking outside the text', *New Statesman*, 9 January.

Denzin, N. (1989) *Interpretative Biography*, London: Sage.

Denzin, N. (1991) 'Deconstructing the biographical method', paper presented at American Educational Research Association Conference, Chicago, 9 April.

Goodson, I.F. (2004) 'Narrative capital and narrative learning', paper given to a workshop at the University of Viborg, November. This paper was considerably extended in doctoral classes given at the University of Barcelona in a course on life stories, during the period January to July 2005.

Goodson, I.F. (2005) *Learning, Curriculum and Life Politics*, London: Routledge.

Lasch, C. (1977) *Haven in a Heartless World*, New York: Basic Books.

McEwan, I. (2005) *Saturday*, London: Penguin.

Menaud, L. (1991) ' "Man of the people", a review of *The True and Only Heaven* by C. Lasch', *New York Review of Books*, *XXXVIII* (7), 11 April.

National Consumer Council (2006) Interview with spokesman on *BBC News*, Thursday 23 March.

O'Hagan, S. (2005) 'Boss class', *Observer Magazine*, 24 April.

Semprun, J. (2004) 'Interview', *Financial Times Weekend*, 27–28 November.

Senge, P. (1990) *The Fifth Discipline: The Art and Practice of the Learning Organization*, New York: Doubleday.

Steinbeck, J. (1939) *The Grapes of Wrath*, New York: Viking Press-James Lloyd.

Troy, G. (1999) *The New York Times*, 24 September.

Williams, H. (2005) Extract from *Chronology of World History*, London: Cassells.

Willinsky, J. (1989) 'Getting personal and practical with personal practical knowledge', *Curriculum Inquiry*, 19, 3.

6 Exploring the teacher's professional knowledge

Constructing identity and community

with Ardra L. Cole

> However peripheral we may be in the lives of others, each of us is always a central point round which the entire world whirls in radiating perspectives.
>
> (Alison Lurie, *Foreign Affairs* 1984)

A starting point for this chapter is a belief that if we are to develop valued models of teacher development, we first need to listen closely to the teacher's voice. We need to continue, almost obsessively, that act of listening. Hence, we feel that the best way to develop sensitive models of professional development is first of all to listen to the professionals at whom the development is aimed. This process of sensitive listening has been advocated at a number of levels recently. For instance, an emerging body of work has recommended the development of collaborative case studies, life stories and narratives which seek to elicit the teacher's 'personal practical knowledge' (e.g. Connelly and Clandinin 1988, 1990) or the teacher's 'pedagogical content knowledge' (Shulman 1986, 1987; Grossman 1990; Gudmundsdottir 1990).

Whilst these approaches make a valuable start in sensitising us to the teacher's voice, they may encourage too partial a view of teachers' knowledge. The research reported herein implies that personal practical knowledge or pedagogical content knowledge is only a part of teachers' 'professional knowledge'. This professional knowledge moves well beyond the personal, practical and pedagogical. To confine it there is to speak in a voice of empowerment, whilst ultimately disempowering. To define teachers' knowledge in terms of its location within the confines of the classroom is to set limits on its potential and use.

Our work points to a range of levels at which teachers' professional knowledge can be discerned. It is certainly true that there is a range of practical and pedagogical knowledge which is of vital importance in understanding the teacher's conduct in classrooms. But alongside that, we have found, there is a range of knowledge of great importance, which deals with the micro-political and contextual realities of school life. Such knowledge is critically important, not least because these micro-political and contextual factors affect the lives and arenas in which personal, practical and pedagogical knowledge are utilised.

 *Teacher narrative*

Background and context

Our study of teachers' professional knowledge and development involved seven full-time instructors newly hired to a community college in south-western Ontario, Canada. The community college system in Canada began during the 1960s and 70s, to meet the growing demands for skilled and technical workers, and to respond to the post-war population explosion. These community colleges are loosely defined as post-secondary, non-degree granting institutions. They are governed by a board of representatives from the local community, and offer programmes reflecting the concerns of the region. The largest college system in Canada is found in Ontario, where there are 23 community colleges serving over 100,000 full-time, post-secondary students and more than 700,000 part-time students.

There are approximately 6,000 full-time faculty employed in the community college system. As a group, college teachers are unique. Almost without exception, teaching is not their first career. Most are hired because of their practical work experience, and they move into the community college setting from some area of business, industry, technology or trade, or from the professions. They receive no formal preparation for their teaching roles, yet they are expected to carry out all the roles and responsibilities associated with being a teacher.

In order to gain a fuller understanding of what it means to become a teacher in a community college, we (Goodson and Cole along with Fliesser, a curriculum consultant at the College) invited a small group of newly hired, full-time community college teachers to join us in a two-year exploration of their experiences, development and socialisation as community college instructors. Like most community college teachers, they joined the faculty 'fresh from the field'. For each, teaching in a community college represented both a career change and a change in professional venue.

The teachers

In this chapter, we focus on Brian and Karen. Brian is an architectural technologist, and Karen is a television production technician.

Studying the socialisation and development of the instructors was particularly interesting because they had not been through any conventional teacher preparation programme; hence, we were able to observe their 'on the job' responses to the new educational workplace. As we followed them through their first two years of teaching, we saw the teachers struggle to define their new role(s) and contexts and to understand themselves as teachers in the community college setting. Although not always articulated explicitly, they seemed to spend much of their induction period searching for answers to questions such as: What does it mean to be a teacher? What does it mean to be part of a new professional community? How do I define the boundaries of my new professional community? How do I become part of that community? To develop an understanding of their answers to these questions and to ground it in a fuller context for each person, we employed the 'life history method' and particularly the 'life history interview' (for a full discussion of life history work see, for example, Goodson 1981).

A note on method

To illustrate our concept of professional knowledge and teacher development, we rely on thoughts, ideas and observations the teachers provided us with, throughout the two-year period. In particular, we draw on information collected in a series of life history interviews with each teacher and bi-weekly group discussions, which took place throughout the period of the study. These group sessions were the major collective milieux for the teachers to voice their views and concerns and express their developing perspectives. Because of our commitment to sponsoring the teacher's voice and learning from what teachers have to say, much of what follows is excerpts from interviews with, and discussions amongst, the teachers. We have tried to keep our commentary to a minimum. Not all of the teachers' voices are heard individually in this chapter, however. We selected excerpts from the life history interviews and group discussions that seemed particularly illustrative of the ideas we advance here. Because the entire group was involved in the bi-weekly discussions, all seven teachers are, in fact, represented frequently, but as a collective voice.

Teacher development, teachers' lives

Teacher development has been characterised in a variety of ways. Fuller and Brown (1975), for example, propose that new teachers progress through a series of concerns-based developmental stages, beginning with actions based on self-centred concerns about survival through to actions based on concerns about students and curricular issues. Ryan (1986) suggests that beginning teachers move through stages of 'fantasy', 'survival', 'mastery' and 'impact'. Burke *et al.* (1984) characterise teacher development in a model of career cycles. Huberman (1989) reflects our own and others' dissatisfaction with such generalised characterisations when he states:

> Modal trends such as these are suspect. Put together, they would probably describe no single individual in [a] sample, and only pieces of subgroups. They are, in fact, normative constructs enabling us to keep analytic order in our minds until we can handle more differentiation and complexity.
>
> (Huberman 1989: 53)

A more recent focus on teachers' lives and personal biographies has consequently led to conceptualisations of teacher development rooted in the 'personal' (e.g. Clandinin 1986; Butt and Raymond 1987; Connelly and Clandinin 1990; Bullough *et al.* 1991; Knowles and Holt-Reynolds 1991). Other studies have argued for a personal mode linked to broader contextual parameters (e.g. Apple 1986;

life history = context

Ball and Goodson 1985; Britzman 1986; Cole 1990; Goodson 1981, 1988, 1989, 1990; Goodson and Walker 1991; Zeichner and Grant 1981; Zeichner and Tabachnick 1985). This chapter seeks to extend this latter view and to provide a story of action within a theory of context.

Toward a broadened perspective in teacher development

Our concept of teacher development is rooted both in the personal and professional. We consider teachers as persons and professionals whose lives and work are shaped by conditions inside and outside of school. Events and experiences, both past and present, that take place at home, school and in the broader social sphere, help to shape teachers' lives and careers. How teachers construe their professional realities and how they carry out their lives in classrooms is an ongoing process of personal and contextual interpretation. In this chapter, we further develop this concept. We move beyond primarily personal, practical and pedagogical notions to define a broader conception of professional knowledge and teacher development, one that places teachers in the broader, micro-political and contextual realities of school life.

In our study of the development and socialisation of seven new community college teachers, a pattern of teacher development emerged, which clearly reflects a transitional quality to the teachers' perceptions of their experiences. We characterise the personal aspect of their development as a struggle to establish professional identity; the context, we characterise in terms of defining boundaries of professional community. Personal/professional development within that personally defined context, we describe in terms of belonging.

Two interlinked analytic foci are employed as we examine these issues of professional development:

1   Constructing professional identities.
2   Constructing professional communities.

Articulating the link between identity and community

To rehearse the interlinked nature of our two analytic themes, we begin with a lengthy passage from an interview with Karen who, at the time, had recently left her job in technical production at a national television station and joined the community college faculty to teach in her area of practical expertise. We quote at length to capture the essence of the link between conceptions of professional identity and professional community.

> KAREN: I started [at the television station] in '78, and two years later was married. [My husband and I] were friends first because we ran in a crew. He was an editor. Everybody on that crew I knew on a first-name basis. I was the one supplying them with the tapes – the gopher. And we would go for lunch together, all of us, so I got to know all of these guys.

IVOR: You were the only female there at the time?

KAREN: Yeah, except for the service secretaries who worked in the scheduling office and who would schedule the shows in the different suites. During the evening shifts we'd go for lunch and then for a beer after the shifts were over at 11:00. [The crew members] became my friends. Some of them had girlfriends, and we sort of got a group going. I started dating Jim. We were married in '82 and bought our house in '83. We had our daughter in '84.

Right after we got married, I switched from videotape to production. I applied to the woman who was in charge of production services, said I would be happy in videotape but I wanted to learn something else and that I would like to get into production. I think I wanted to use more creativity. The videotape was creative but you were also pushing the buttons for somebody beside you. They would assign a producer to come in who would say, 'Okay, cut this item and edit this item.' He/she would sit beside you and say, 'Edit there. Let's put this music on.' It was a little frustrating. So I thought, 'Well, I'll go to [the production] side and see what that's like for a while. Since I know the editing it might help.' So I went into production and was offered a job.

First of all you have to go through another training, first as a script assistant and then a production assistant. The script assistant is in the control room timing the shows. It tended to be a little more clerical than I would have liked. I'm not a clerical type of person but I certainly learned how to time a show – I did [two news programmes] – and I certainly know the feeling of going live with a new show. It is very exciting.

Everything is [trade] unions [at the station] so everything is classified at union scale. Going from videotape to production was essentially a lateral move but since there are just three [job classification] groups in production, I just moved up to the third group.

ARDRA: So you were in the top group?

KAREN: Yeah, the top of the script assistant group. And then, I worked on [an afternoon news and information show] where I became what they call a service producer. Because of budget cuts you didn't get any extra money for it but the job function was still there and they still trained people for it. I liked doing it so I didn't really care about the money.

I was kind of a producer who oversees the videotape department. It was a perfect setting for me because it was production; yet, I was in the videotape department with all the old guys, the gang. My job was basically organising and coordinating the whole videotape department for that whole particular show. You were there in the morning until it was off-air and then you go back and prepare for the next day. And that's where I was when we left in June '88.

ARDRA: Where was Jim?

KAREN: Jim was an editor, one of the top editors. Then he started with [a national prime-time news show]. When we got married in '82, I went to production. At the same time he went to [the news show] which was, at that time, quite a separate section of videotape. Supposedly, the 'elite' editors went to work on that show because it was a new show with new equipment. They had to do a lot more work and they became more production editors/directors doing a lot more than straight editing. He stayed with [that show] until we left. He was there for seven years.

It was the winter of '87 when we started thinking about leaving. I was getting sick of [the afternoon show] but there wasn't a job to go to next. It was like the ladder was chopped off, and there wasn't anything I could see to go to. I could have gone into a producer's job but the work was not any more challenging. And it wasn't a move up either. It wasn't any more money. It wasn't any more prestige. It was just another job. It didn't interest me. Management was the only other area and, since managers are a dime a dozen, there just wasn't any little niche that I could see that I wanted to go into.

So work was getting a little depressing and we were getting just a little stagnated there. Although my husband was happy on [the news show] – the people were good, he loved the show, loved the equipment – his boss was from the old department and there was a rivalry going between him and the supervisor of the other department. So there were a lot of morale problems, back-stabbing, and some terrible things that went on that just ruined it for some of the people there.

It was just a time when Jim was getting frustrated with the politics of the corporation – mostly the politics, not anything else. And I was getting sick and tired because there wasn't anything else to go into. There weren't any new shows then. I mean a new show would have been great 'cause I would have been starting all over again.

(Interview, August 1989)

As is illustrated in the above case with Karen, the teachers entered the community college setting with already well-developed concepts, both of professional community and professional identity – antecedents to the new notions of professional context and identity they would develop. After ten years, Karen, for example, left the community of visual broadcasting. Whilst there, she had developed strong personal and professional ties, gained considerable knowledge of the political workings of the corporation and acquired experience and expertise in her area of work. Beginning at the bottom rung, she had worked her way up the corporate ladder until it 'was chopped off'. In her reading of her work context, she did not see further possibilities for the kind of creative expression and professional autonomy she needed. And so, yearning for a new challenge, Karen opted for a change and to become part of a new professional community of community college teachers.

Changing professional roles/career and moving into a new professional community initiated a process of redefinition. In a period of transition and adjustment, Karen and the others had to reconstruct their notions of professional self-identity and develop new understandings about their new workplace community. As we followed them through this process, trying to make sense of the personal/professional reconstruction which took place, an image of expanding concentric circles presented itself to us. As we listened to and talked with the teachers, we picked up a clear sense of outward movement, both conceptually in terms of how they defined their new role(s) within the new work context and physically, as they became more involved in activities outside their own classrooms. They seemed to keep pushing back the boundaries of their thinking about what it means to be a teacher in a community college, as well as the boundaries that defined their work community.

The boundaries that initially defined the teachers' personal conceptions of community were narrow and tight. In the beginning, the professional milieu was the classroom. Over time, this notion was broadened to encompass an increasing amount of territory outside the classroom until, finally, the teachers' concept of community included the community college venue in a broad sense. Similarly, the process of redefining professional self-identity first involved a gradual shift from seeing oneself as primarily defined by the previous occupation, to seeing oneself as a teacher. And within the new conceptual frame, the teachers gradually expanded their ideas about what it means to be a teacher. For the remainder of the chapter, we deal separately with these two analytical foci.

Constructing professional identities

For each teacher, qualitative shifts in self-perception occurred over time. They entered the community college not thinking of themselves as teachers. Each had an antecedent professional identity rooted in a previous professional context. A progressive change, both in breadth and depth, was evidenced in the individual interviews, and in the group discussions, as the participants came to define and redefine their roles and see themselves as teachers. Excerpts from two of the life history interviews provide examples of how the teachers began teaching; not yet 'feeling like teachers', not thinking about themselves as teachers. These interviews took place prior to, or at the start of, the first term of the first year.

> KAREN: The thought of teaching [at the time of a first career decision] was 'Teaching what? What do I teach?' Teaching students, standing up in front of the class. I mean I just didn't see it as the job I wanted to do.
>
> I can't think like a teacher yet. I can't look at a calendar and say: 'Mid-terms are worth this percentage; 25% have to be of written marks; and, when am I going to write a test?' I haven't put together tests yet or projects or figured out how many weeks [I have to work with]. I mean, I keep looking at the calendar and going, 'How many weeks are in this semester?' I haven't thought yet in that thought process as a teacher as far as long-term planning of curriculum ... I think obviously after one year I'll be able to say, 'Well, that didn't work. I'm throwing that out next year and I'm going to add this and shorten this and lengthen that

and maybe spend more time doing this.' Then I'll know, but right now it's ...

(Interview, August 1989)

BRIAN. [When I started] I thought I felt like a teacher – a teacher of architectural technology – because I had learned [the content of] what I had to teach. I'd been in the industry for a number of years so I felt I had something. I felt confident in my position. I'm not saying I felt like a teacher yet. But I felt confident in my position [with regard to content expertise].

(Interview, September 1989)

Initially, the teachers seemed to be striving towards goals of improved practice based on a narrow and technical view of teaching, their implicit assumption being: 'I have the content knowledge so I will be a teacher once I master certain technical skills for its delivery.' In the early group discussions, facilitated by the curriculum consultant at the college, the teachers focused their conversations on the technical aspects of teaching. Excerpts from our field notes illustrate:

The group explored possible ways of handling difficult students. There was further discussion on how to handle missed assignments. Brian raised a question about the appropriate use of overhead transparencies, a topic which precipitated much discussion. This led to further talk about the use of handouts and other teaching aids.

(Field notes, September 1989)

There was almost a unanimous concern about time and organization. Lecture preparation and text construction were seen as especially time consuming ... Karen expressed concern about how to coordinate groups within the classroom. She is also trying to individualise instruction but is having trouble figuring out what she needs to teach them by a given time.

(Field notes, October 1989)

Qualitative shifts in thinking, however, occurred over time. As the following two passages indicate, changes in the nature and content of the group discussions indicated an ongoing redefinition of the teachers' ideas on what it means to teach. We can interpret a shift to a focus on curricular issues, the teaching–learning process and discussions of different teaching philosophies, as the teachers begin to see themselves as pedagogues rather than as mere technicians. These field notes were taken during two group discussions held in the first year, one at the end of the first term and the other at the beginning of the second term:

Ann offered to share a bit about what was going on in her class. The students were doing presentations which, she said, were going very well. But she wanted to know how to take the presentations one step further so that all the students could build on them. In other words, how could the presentations be used as a teaching–learning tool? 'How can I teach *with* [the students] rather than *to* them?'

(Field notes, December 1989)

The subject shifted to evaluating students in cooperative learning situations. Brian offered to share some of his ideas about using peer evaluation as a team-building activity. A lot of suggestions about using group work and cooperative learning were made. Then Ann posed a question about the role of the teacher in an independent learning situation. The discussion turned to the issue of the image of the teacher – as director, teller, facilitator. They all seem to be struggling with their image of what a teacher is, what their classrooms should be, and what their role is in the classroom. Brian offered his perspective that in spite of the initial tendency to want to 'teach', it's okay to 'guide'.

(Field notes, January 1990)

The following passages, from an interview with Karen midway through her first year, are particularly illustrative of the re-identification process. She reflects on how her thinking about teaching has changed, articulates some of her developing conceptions about her role and looks forward to further change and role expansion over time.

> KAREN: I thought I was teaching because I was knowledgeable about television and that's what I was teaching. Whenever I'd say the word 'teaching', in the back of my head I'd still think, 'me teaching?' Friends would say 'You're a teacher?' Everybody thinks back to their teachers in high school or elementary or university. And that would throw me for a while. But then after a while I thought, 'Yeah, I'm here because I know what I'm talking about.'
>
> When I was hired I was excited. I got a job teaching in a college. [I thought] 'This is the career of a lifetime.' It's something I never imagined doing. And it was perfect. It was exactly what I needed to do or wanted to do. I never thought of it like, 'Yes, I wanted to be a college teacher some day.' Yet, it was the accumulation of my television background ... I'm a people person. And I like to move and talk and generate ideas, and to get people going. I just like the whole atmosphere [of teaching and learning]. You see a product at the end. I like working hard but I also like to see something completely accomplished at the end. And this was the perfect job where that all would come to be. When I started it was, 'I'm a teacher! I'm a teacher! I'm a teacher! I can't believe it!' My husband and everybody would joke about it. It was like, 'I can't believe that I got this job. It's the chance of a lifetime!'
>
> Now, [the idea of being a teacher] is not important to me any more. It's important that [the students] are learning something from me. And

that it's fun and it's encouraging. Maybe I'll [change my mind later on] but at this point every day is different. So to me that's the ideal job.

That's what most people complain about. They come home after a while and their job is mundane. Nothing changes. [Teaching] is something in which you see the accomplishment at the end of the day. Some days you come home and you're a little frustrated. It didn't go the way you want. The next day it's either a different group of faces or the same faces but a different situation. And one person comes up to you and says, 'Yeah, I got that. I'm going to do this and this.' You think, 'I got to that person. I really got to that person and it meant something.'

I want these students to come back after a couple of years when they get jobs and say, 'You know you really helped me.' I hope they will say that 'I had a good time at college and I really learned a lot. You were encouraging.' So, I think that's more important now to me than it was the first couple of months. The first months I was still on that cloud about what I was doing – a little nervous, but now I'm not nervous any more.

I don't think [some of the older, more experienced teachers] get to know the students. I think they get to a point where they have a curriculum to follow and they teach to a class, not to individuals. By not getting to know the individuals – and I don't mean really personally, I just mean getting to know their irks and how they're motivated or how they're not motivated – you don't see the ones who don't think highly of themselves and that you have to give a little extra pat on the back or whatever. By not focusing on those individuals the classroom becomes 'cattle going in, cattle going out'.

I'm changing. I should say changing the programme but I don't want to make it sound that large-scale. I mean changing things that I see haven't worked. I've been through that course [as a student at the same college] and it hasn't changed and now I'm saying, 'Okay, can we update it a little bit?' And [the other instructors] are very receptive which is something I never imagined possible.

I thought that coming in as the low person on the totem pole [the implicit rules would be]: 'Learn. Watch where you walk. And don't step on any toes.' But it's not like that. That's exciting for me because to me, that's part of the job as well – if you have the time.

ARDRA: Your involvement in the extra-curricular activities, things that take you outside the classroom, is that part of your teacher role?

KAREN: Some are. Some are political. When someone asks me to do something I'm the type that usually says, 'Oh yeah, I'll do it.' I always take on too much but I'm also in a position where I would like to do other things. Eventually, I'd like to coordinate our programme so the more I learn about the different aspects – the budgeting process for programmes and things like that – the more knowledge I'll have. So I'm enjoying that.

> I think one of the things I'm enjoying is that our coordinator is very receptive to change. He wants to revamp the programme, to keep it current. And he hasn't had a lot of feedback or encouragement from other colleagues as yet. Most of the other colleagues are close to retirement and the one I replaced actually was very resistant to change. I think [the coordinator] sees the potential for some new ideas because I'm new in the industry. And I didn't expect that.
>
> I really thought that I would be the low person on the totem pole. 'This is what we're doing. We'll help you out and show you some things but take a little bit at a time.' Instead I'm getting, 'Have you got any ideas? Can we do this? How do you want to change it?' There's more power there, more freedom to do things that I never thought I would be able to do. We're talking about revamping the whole year next year and they're going on my idea. I think, 'Wow, this is exciting. It's very encouraging.'
>
> (Interview, January 1990)

Karen was clear in her initial conception of teaching as delivery of content knowledge. She was less certain about her identity as teacher. She experienced initial discomfort/confusion over having the label 'teacher' attached to her – not certain that it fit. She was, however, euphoric over the opportunities for creative expression and accomplishment that she thought her new role would provide. Soon, Karen accepted the 'teacher' label and began to develop her understandings about the role(s) associated with that label. She began to identify success and satisfaction in terms of her ability to facilitate students' learning. Later, she expanded the criteria to include her ability to effect programme change.

Along with the expanding conceptions of teaching came increasing role complexity and a related need to develop new knowledge. Content knowledge was no longer sufficient to carry out the multiple and complex roles Karen was adopting. She also recognised the need for knowledge of herself as a teacher; the students as individuals; how to best facilitate their learning; curriculum (beyond content knowledge); and how to effect programme change in her own class and department. Essentially, she was experiencing and demonstrating a need for personal, practical, pedagogical *and* professional knowledge of the micro-political context.

The following passages further illustrate how the teachers changed their perceptions of their role to extend beyond the technical and pedagogical to the institutional. They began to see themselves as contributing members of a department, designing institutional strategies.

ANN: You know, personally I can do things creatively with my kids in the classroom but that's not all there is to it. It's wider than that. I feel as if we've got a stake, or I've got a stake, in looking at changing our early childhood education field. There's been a movement for probably about the last ten years to recognise the child as a child. It's against that whole notion of 'the hurried child' – the disappearance of childhood if you like. When I think of young four-month-old babies going into care, I think we need to address some of those aspects of how that affects that child long term. 'What sort of programme do we want that child be in when they're with us eight or nine hours a day? And what should that programme look like?'

The expectation for the child entering grade one is that the child knows colours, and reading and writing skills for readiness. We used to talk about that for grade one. So the Kindergarten then adjusts their programme to meet what the grade one needs. If you look at Junior Kindergarten, we're talking about three-year-olds who are now being pushed into that situation for readiness. We're saying, 'No, just a minute. The child at that age needs to develop in all areas. This is not just an intellectual approach.'

And so here we've got almost a new movement which is child-centred. All our texts reflect it but some of our practice in the field doesn't. So we have some dissention among [the community college] people. We're trying to move from that traditional look at what the teacher knows best to what the child needs. And the reason we're looking at the child's needs is because of that potential institutionalisation of children from the age of four months up.

It's scary! I think those are some of the issues that we need to deal with and we're not. There are a couple of us who are on the same wavelength. We're not saying that this is something new. This is not new. It's not that we've suddenly thought this up and we're going to try and mix the pot here. Other community colleges have a child-centred approach in place. We now want the curriculum to fit the child rather than the child to fit the curriculum. And that's where the clash is, I think.

If you really believe in child development, how can you not acknowledge the development? In the private sector, when I'm talking about education, I would have far more response to our innovative ideas than I do in the teaching institution which I anticipated would be full of innovative ideas and creativity. If we don't have it here, where is it?

And then I hear people saying, 'Well, you know, we can't tell the community college what to do.' Somebody has to start somewhere. It's not my approach [to be directive]. I'm much more persuasive. But give me a chance to persuade. Give me a forum to persuade and I'll do it [laughs].

(Interview, May 1991)

As time went on, there was less and less talk about the technical aspects of teaching (other than as a term of reference for growth) and increasing attention to concerns about how to effect substantive change within and outside the classroom. Broadly stated, the teachers expanded their conceptions of teaching and themselves as teachers from an early image of the teacher as classroom technician to one of the teacher as agent of change.

KAREN: The people in my department are very congenial. It's very small. There's only a coordinator and another full-time colleague and myself. They both were my teachers when I took the course there so it was a bit strange at first. But it's worked out very well. They're a good group and we get along very well. They were very good. They were very support-ive. I just stood back and was quiet for a while. And now of course I never shut up [laughs]. Now I try to take over [laughs].

Our coordinator is a very positive person, very enthusiastic. He's will-ing to take any ideas that I have and go with them. He wants the course to change but he just has no idea what to do. So that is good for me. I have to watch it too. I can be very political. But it's very enthusiastic for me because I've been able to do a lot of things and change a lot of things. A lot of people just sit back or sit on the fence but I'll go for it.

Maybe I'm having a lot more political freedom in our department than in some of the others as far as changing things, just because things haven't been changed for a long time. They want the change. They know they have to keep up but they've been there so long they don't know what to do. So, it's not just teaching, it's revamping the whole thing. In 10 years they're going to be retired and there will be other new teachers coming in. I want it to go in a way that I can see working there still in 15 years. So that's been really good for me.

Some of the things my coordinator said 'we' would do, the two of us. I don't know what happened but he kind of took a step back and I was standing alone.

(Interview, April 1991)

To summarise the teachers' development of self-identity, we once again turn to the teachers themselves. Karen and Brian describe their development of 'self as teacher' in this way:

KAREN: I don't really know when it clicked or when it happened. It just seemed to assimilate. I remember that first interview the day before I went to teach the first day. I remember thinking, 'I can't believe I'm a teacher.' I'd pinch myself, 'Gee, I'm working at a college. This is ridicu-lous.' And then it's just kind of come about so that now it's almost like, 'Oh yeah, no big deal.'

[The transition to teaching is] not as scary as I thought it would be. It was a lot more stimulating than I thought it would be. You just start thinking like a teacher, talking like a teacher. Throughout the year I found I was constantly [collecting information related to teaching]. Anything I read I think, 'Oh yeah, that's great. That's great, I could use that. Or I could do that.' [The same thing applies] if I hear about somebody using some other method. And you start automatically apply-ing everything that comes in. You kind of put ideas about methods and things on that teaching shelf so that you can use them. And you just start thinking about making yourself a better teacher. It just kind of happens. You just kind of evolve and just start thinking that way. I never imagined it would be that easy to transform into a teacher. But it's something that just starts to come comfortably.

(Interview, May 1990)

BRIAN: I have a lot better idea of what a teacher does than I did at the beginning. At the beginning I thought, 'How hard can it be?' I mean you just stand up and you talk, and you show them how it's done. How hard can that be? And now I know how hard it can be.

ARDRA: It's no longer just standing up and talking?

BRIAN: It's just nuts. I mean there's a lot more involved in being a good teacher. [You need] to know your material and how to present the material. There are a lot of people who know their material inside out, but if they can't get it across to other people so that the people can walk away and understand it ... And then [you need] the ability to know how to use a classroom to its best abilities, and what works best in presenting that material. And then, after the material is presented, how to evaluate it, how to evaluate the students, and their abilities to understand.

There is a lot more to teaching than just standing up in front of people and talking. At the beginning I didn't think there was. You also can't teach something unless you understand it.

ARDRA: So the complex roles of the teacher are sort of presenting themselves to you as you...

BRIAN: And again, at the beginning, teaching was, 'Oh, they're all the same. They're students. They want to learn architectural technology.' They're not all the same. Some of them need more time. And there are other issues on hand for the student now that I need to take into consideration. A part-time job seems to be a big thing, a necessity these days in order to go to school.

In my first year I was saying to my students, 'Well no, it's either school or work. You can't do both.' I didn't mean it as an ultimatum. And now you talk to some of these people and literally the part-time job is what's putting food on their table and paying their rent, because [assistance funds] didn't come through or whatever. So I'm not as harsh about it. Now, instead of, 'No, you can't have a part-time job', it's, 'Okay, but just make sure you schedule your hours appropriately. Make sure you have the time to do the work.' I'm more supportive of those [situations] rather than harsh and judgemental.

And now I think [teaching] is much more complex. The one and only time I walked into a classroom unprepared taught me that lesson. I was very busy and just didn't have the chance to fully prepare. I had an outline of what I wanted to do but I didn't have things down pat the way I should have. That taught me never again [to be unprepared]. It was really embarrassing and difficult. And I felt as if I really cheated the students, and that didn't sit well with me. So I never did that again.

ARDRA: Since you came on full-time a couple of years ago almost, do you see that your role has changed very much?

BRIAN: I look at myself as a teacher and that's my job.

ARDRA: You didn't in the beginning? [laughs]

BRIAN: No. No. But now I do. I guess my attitudes have changed. I wasn't quite sure that I was a teacher. Yeah, I guess that's right, when I look back on it.

ARDRA: You think of yourself as a teacher. Do you still think of yourself though as an architectural technologist?

BRIAN: Oh yes, but not as much. I still think of myself as an architectural technologist because that was my choice of profession. But what I'm doing now is instead of practising it, and I do still practise it, but I'm now a teacher. So, I'm a teacher of architectural technology. And I feel a lot more comfortable now than I did two years ago.

(Interview, May 1991)

And so, as the teachers reflect on their transition to teaching, their metamorphosis seems complete. The initial discomfort with the idea of identifying themselves as teachers no longer exists. Brian's final comments reflect the sentiments of the entire group. With an acknowledgement of their 'first choice of profession', they now talk about themselves, not in terms of their previous roles in their respective fields, but as teachers. They seem to have achieved a level of comfort in the development of their professional identity as teachers, which approximates to that previously defined within the earlier professional/vocational context.

Constructing professional communities

Using a similar representational process, we now turn to our second focus and, once again, rely on the teachers to illustrate the concept of 'constructing professional communities'. We remind the reader of our image of the ever-widening circle of development, and begin with the teachers' initial and somewhat narrowly defined view of 'classroom as professional community'. Returning to the discussions and interviews held at the beginning of the first year, once again we follow the teachers through their first two years. The teachers' initial understandings of what teachers do, and where roles are played out, were bounded by the classroom walls. An analysis of field notes on the first two group sessions – held in the early part of the first term in the first year – reveals a focus on topics/concerns that relate intimately to the classroom: managing time; preparing lesson plans; interpreting curriculum guidelines and developing new curriculum; long-range planning; individualised instruction; lesson presentation; and use of audiovisual equipment and aids.

At some point late in the first term, there was evidence of an initial qualitative shift in the nature and content of the group discussions. The following examples show how conversation began to, and continued to, move beyond the classroom walls. Boundaries were extended; walls were pushed back; the circle widened to encompass a greater territory.

KAREN: I think the answer, at least for our department, is to try to get more industry involved in community colleges, whether it be sponsorship of private companies or just industries that are going to benefit from our graduates. I think it may take some marketing on our part as individuals in our divisions or in the college as a whole. But we need to try to say, 'Look, we are putting these students out and we're giving you something. We need something back.' And it can't just be the government. They can't be the only one funding right now.

We have to look at ourselves as public relations people and sales people, as well as teachers, if we want our departments to keep up. To keep up with the level that we need to teach [we need] to keep up with the industry. And industry is also going to have to give back what they get out. I think we've got to get that across to them that we can't just keep churning out students. If we can't keep up, those students we're churning out are becoming less and less qualified.

Industry can afford to keep up because they have profits to prove it. We have to say, 'Well, you've got to give what we give. You have to help us produce these students who are up to date and excellent.' That way you also generate more students coming into the system – if they can see an end, if they can see something that is a goal worth going after. But I think we have to actively start doing something.

(Group discussion, December 1989)

ANN: There's a lot of money going in. I think that one of the problems is a question of where that money is going and what it's going for. I can see we may have a new building going up out there which is going to be very beneficial but it really depends on how the whole thing is operated. We asked if we could have our offices out there or if we would have close ties with that new building [but we were told]. 'No, we'd have to stay up in our own building.' In [another community college] the whole early childhood department is all part of that whole building. They have direct access to the resource rooms and things like that going on right there. The sad part is that we're building that beautiful building out there and here we are still over here.

(Group discussion, December 1989)

As the year progressed and the teachers became more settled in their new professional milieux, we began to see increasing evidence of an interest in departmental activity.

KAREN: In May and June I'm going to work on changing the evaluation. I can do whatever I want. I find [the current method] very awkward. I would prefer to do my own and have [the other instructor] go and do his own, and then take the average of the two because I happened to get to know the students earlier. He just found he didn't know all the faces. Now he does tend to let me do most of the marking but to me it's a waste of time. We have 30 students to go through and it's probably about 20 minutes per student to do this. It doesn't sit well with me. So it's been left that I can change it in May.

(Group discussion, March 1990)

The teachers' increasing involvement in activities outside the classroom was further evidenced in a group discussion that took place early in the second term of the first year. The topic of a pre-session conversation was their involvement in extra-curricular activities. Karen talked about her key role in the production of a video related to community college activities, to be shown on a local television station. Bill commented on some culinary competitions in which he had become involved in support of the students. Jim had taken on extra responsibilities related to the provision of in-service training on a recently implemented policy affecting work environment.

As time passed, the teachers continued to express a growing interest in life beyond the classroom walls. A further significant shift occurred during another discussion that took place early in the second term of year one, where an interest was expressed in learning the micro-politics of the institution: how things work; how things get done; how to make changes. Again, we quote from our field notes:

An interesting sequence of events took place here. Linda spoke about the 'politics of the institution'. She talked about the constraints, the road blocks to change, and the need to acquire early insight into the politics of an institution in order to bring about any change. Ann shared her expertise and knowledge about collegiality in the college and issues of power and control in relation to status in programme design and development. Brian brought up the notion of the need for new people to conform. 'Otherwise,' he said, 'they're not wanted.'

This is the first time there has been such an informed and lively discussion around the issue of institutional politics and the need to be aware of and learn institutional norms as part of the whole socialisation process. It will be interesting to watch that develop. We are half-way through year one now. Before, there wasn't much interest beyond the walls of the classroom. Now we are starting to see the classroom walls being pushed back.

(Field notes, January 1990)

The teachers continued to ask questions that took them farther afield from the classroom – questions about budget, how to make curricular changes and how to strengthen links with industry and the community beyond the college. As time went on, there was even less, indeed very little, talk situated in or confined to the classroom. A good illustration of this point is found in the first group session of the second year. The first part of this meeting was spent planning session topics for the year. The teachers generated a list of possible topics and then placed them in order of priority. Institutional micro-politics was ranked number one and classroom-specific issues came up last!

> Karen made a request that really changed the whole nature of the discussion. She requested information or a workshop session on school–community relations, particularly on funding issues. I think this is a critical incident in her development and certainly in the development of the teachers, considering the response she received to that request. Here we see the teachers pushing back the classroom walls even further, wanting to move out into the community and trying to establish, maintain and encourage school-community links.
>
> Karen commented, 'Last year I was just worried about teaching. Now I'm interested in changing the programme.' A very critical statement, I think. 'How do we get things to change?' she asked. Karen talked about her growing interest in learning how the system works and how to get things done. 'Perhaps,' she said, 'someone from [the college] could explain how [the college] works.' There was a lively discussion and no more suggestions after this.
>
> After a rank-ordering of the five topics suggested for workshop sessions, it came down to a decision between 'micropolitics' and a workshop on group work for the first to be held. There was consensus, in the end, that micropolitics was definitely the topic of interest, especially over the long term. It was perceived to be quite essential. Particularly, there was interest in budgeting – how the budget works and how decisions are made.
>
> (Field notes, September 1991)

The boundaries of community continued to be extended; the circle ever widened. In most of the last individual interviews and certainly in the final group discussion of the second year, the entire talk was located in the broader community college venue. Often the teachers returned to their previous experiences of occupational community and drew parallels between the previous and present contexts. And so, after a two-year period of induction/socialisation to a new professional venue, the teachers, for the most part, had developed a concept of community that has degrees of continuity with that defined within the previous vocational context. As with Karen:

> It makes me feel slightly disappointed. I think, at any job when you start you think, 'This is going to be it. This is going to be wonderful.' And, all of a sudden, reality sets in and you say, 'You know, there are the same problems in every job. Whether you're a carpenter, or whether you're in the education field, or whether you're in the television field, the same problems are there. Some people do the job well and you have to work with those people.'

I'm a little surprised in that I didn't expect there to be a lack of interest [among the senior colleagues] in their own professional development. I just assumed that you would always want to be better, especially in the education field, because there are new minds coming in every year and it's such a changing field. Because you're teaching, that field is constantly growing but also because you're being challenged every year from young minds and different people. You're not around the same people. I would think that you would want to be constantly on the ball and that everybody would naturally be gung-ho. There are people who may not be as excited about [ongoing professional development]. I guess I'm surprised that there's no push for it to continue.

When I got my first job after I graduated from college, I knew I wanted to be in television. I used to tell myself I wanted to be a producer because I like making decisions. I like organising and I like working with a large group of people. I do like being the boss, if you'd like to put it that way, not for the title so much, but because when I have an idea I see working, I have to be the boss to see it followed through. And that's what I used to think I wanted to do.

So I saw this job – after being in television and not necessarily being the producer – as an opportunity to make decisions that had some meaning, that had some influence on other people's lives, that people could benefit from – not like with a television show where they would say, 'Well, that was a good show but it's gone.' But maybe someone would say, 'That was a great teacher' or, 'That was a great course I took.'

(Interview, January 1991)

Facilitating teacher development

As we followed the teachers through their transition period, it became apparent that the process of redefining what it means to be a teacher and their developing sense of new professional identity were contextually dependent on their developing notions of professional community. This leads us to suspect that in order for teachers to have opportunities to realise their individually defined personal/ professional potential, teaching and development need to be defined, interpreted and facilitated within a broader institutional context. When, in the context of professional development, the boundaries of a teacher's professional community are pushed back to encompass the entire workplace context and attention is paid to the micro-political and contextual realities of school life, it seems to us that teachers have a better chance of becoming truly empowered. In other words, teacher development, in its broadest sense, depends on teachers having access to professional knowledge beyond just the personal, practical and pedagogical.

It is in the broader institutional arenas that the teachers see both major frustrations and the possibilities for significant change. The frustration and anger about 'the system' becomes a rising tide within the transcripts of the meetings.

Take the following statement by Jim, who describes his new job as a 'dream come true':

> I love my job, I really do, but constantly institutional politics intercede. People trying to build empires with hidden agendas and all the bullshit shouldn't be getting in the way between me and the student. It ticks me right off. I've never been good at politics. I don't want to be good at politics. I just want to do the damned job. But it gets to the point where it's almost impossible to be able to do it properly.
>
> There are people who just do what they want to do and that's it. It keeps them happy. Sometimes it's bloody sad. In fact, to me, that's depressing because that spark of enthusiasm just gets smaller and smaller and smaller. And in the end it's going to be extinguished. What do you do? Do you fight the system until you just end up on the floor or do you roll along with it?
>
> (Discussion, May 1991)

In this quote, and indeed within the testimonies quoted within this chapter, we see the richness of pursuing detailed accounts of the life histories of teachers. The grounding of our data in these historical contexts, both personal and micropolitical, offers alternative insights into pedagogical and curricular rationales. At least as importantly, the eloquence of the teachers' voices exhorts us to develop new modes of teacher education, which give new respect to the personal and political realities of teachers' lives.

We recognise that, in exposing the reader to a good deal of unedited transcripts of teachers' voices, we have imposed an extra task. So much of our research normally comprises the researcher's commentary – it may therefore appear almost a 'dereliction of duty' to provide so much 'raw data' and so little commentary. But research paradigms and our expectations of them are social constructs. Moreover, they are social constructs that have, unwittingly or not, silenced teachers' voices and teachers' lives. The process of rehabilitating teachers' voices is likely to be painstaking and contested. It is not by chance that paradigms have silenced the teacher, but without such rehabilitation we believe much of the research on teachers will continue to be arid and decontextualised; irrelevant for the teachers it so systematically silences and disenfranchises. As we have written elsewhere:

> The kind of theory we are searching for would not be the sole prerogative of the university scholar. Our educational study should be more collaborative, more broad-based, publicly available. But it should be possible too for us to make it interesting, critical, vital and useful.
>
> (Goodson and Walker 1991: 203–4)

This chapter marks our tentative search for such a mode of study and reportage in work that is currently underway. We recognise that we are at the first stage of a long journey. Behind this journey, however, lies a clear value position that embraces the notion of the teacher as potentially the central change in restructuring schooling. To quote from Lawrence Stenhouse's memorial plaque, 'It is teachers who, in the end, will change the world of the school by understanding it.'

References

Apple, M. (1986) *Teachers and Texts*, London: Routledge and Kegan Paul.

Ball, S.J. and Goodson, I.F. (eds) (1985) *Teachers' Lives and Careers*, London: Falmer Press.

Britzman, D. (1986) 'Cultural myths in the making of a teacher: biography and social structure in education', *Harvard Educational Review*, 56, 442–56.

Bullough, R.V., Jr, Knowles, J.G. and Crow, N.A. (1991) *Emerging as a Teacher*, London: Routledge Kegan.

Burke, P.J., Fessler, R. and Christensen, J.C. (1984) *Teacher Career Stages: Implications for Staff Development*, Bloomington: Phi Delta Kappa Educational Foundation.

Butt, R.L. and Raymond, D. (1987) 'Arguments for using qualitative approaches in understanding teacher thinking: the case for biography', *Journal for Curriculum Theorizing*, 7(2), 62–93.

Clandinin, D.J. (1986) *Classroom Practice: Teacher Images in Action*, Barcombe Lewes: Falmer Press.

Cole, A.L. (1990) 'Teachers' experienced knowledge: a continuing study', paper presented at the Annual Meeting of the American Educational Research Association, Boston, (April), RIE# ED318733.

Connelly, F.M. and Clandinin, D.J. (1988) *Teachers as Curriculum Planners: narratives of experience*, New York: Teachers College Press.

Connelly, F.M. and Clandinin, D.J. (1990) 'Stories of experience and narrative inquiry', *Educational Researcher*, 14(5), 2–14.

Fuller, F.F. and Brown, O.H. (1975) 'Becoming a teacher', *Teacher Education*, Seventy-Fourth Yearbook of the National Society for the Study of Education, Chicago: University of Chicago Press.

Goodson, I.F. (1981) 'Life histories and studies of schooling', *Interchange*, 11(14), 62–76.

Goodson, I.F. (1988) *The Making of Curriculum: Collected Essays*, London: Falmer Press.

Goodson, I.F. (1989) 'Sponsoring the teacher's voice', *Cambridge Journal of Education*, 21(1), 35–45.

Goodson, I.F. (1990) 'Studying curriculum: towards a social constructionist prospective', *Journal of Curriculum Studies*, 22, 299–312.

Goodson, I.F. and Walker, R. (1991) *Biography, Identity and Schooling*, London: Falmer Press.

Grossman, P. (1990) 'What are we talking about anyway? Subject matter knowledge of secondary English teachers', in J. Brophy (ed.) *Advances in Research on Teaching, Vol. 2: Teachers' Knowledge of Subject Matter as it Relates to their Teaching Practice*, Greenwich: JAI Press.

Gudmundsdottir, S. (1990) 'Values in pedagogical context knowledge', *Journal of Teacher Education*, 41, 3.

Huberman, M. (1989) 'The professional life cycle of teachers', *Teachers College Record*, 91(1), 31–51.

Knowles, J.G. (1992) 'Models for understanding preservice and beginning teachers' biographies: illustrations from case studies', in I. Goodson (ed.) *Studying Teachers' Lives*, London: Routledge.

Knowles, J.G., and Holt-Reynolds, D. (1991) 'Shaping pedagogies through personal histories in preservice teacher education', *Teachers College Record*, 93(1), 87–113.

Lurie, A. (1984) *Foreign Affairs*, US: Random House.

Ryan, K. (1986) 'The Induction of New Teachers', a report for Delta Kappa Educational Foundation, Bloomington, Indiana.

Shulman, L.S. (1986) 'Those who understand: knowledge growth in teaching', *Educational Researcher*, 15, 4–14.

Shulman, L.S. (1987) 'Knowledge and teaching: foundations of the new reform', *Harvard Educational Review*, 57(1), 1–22.

Zeichner, K.M. and Grant, C. (1981) 'Biography and social structure in the socialization of student teachers: a reexamination of the pupil control ideologies of student teachers', *Journal of Education for Teaching*, 3, 299–314.

Zeichner, K.M. and Tabachnick, B.R. (1985) 'The development of teacher perspectives: social strategies and institutional control in the socialization of beginning teachers', *Journal of Education for Teaching*, 11, 1–25.

7 Listening to professional life stories

Some cross-professional perspectives

In pursuing an understanding of teachers' lives and careers, I have focused on an individual life story to highlight some contemporary themes. A number of these themes have been recently elucidated in the Professional Network Report (2002–8) covering seven European countries. These themes can be easily uncovered in a wide range of places and in all of the caring professions of the public services. In the past few years, I have had the opportunity to travel extensively and to interview a varied set of professional workers.

It is important to situate one understanding of teachers' lives and careers in a general context of professional settings. Often these life narrative insights are a cross-professional phenomenon common not just to teachers, but to most public service workers.

A few vignettes might provide confirmation of the general nature of the responses, later epitomised by the teachers. First, a group of young British nurses talking to me at great length about how the new focus on targets and league tables for hospitals takes them away from the vocation they entered nursing for:

> I came into nursing because, all my life – well, since I can remember – I have wanted to look after people and care for them. It's something I grew up with in my family: my grandma was a midwife and my mum a part-time orderly. So you could say it was in the blood. I'm not a squeamish person and blood and vomit and poo have never put me off, if I can get to care for the person who is in the frontline of pain, namely the patient. Some fools in the Health Trusts now call them 'clients' – bloody silly if you ask me! But for me, looking after patients and talking to them, treating them and making them comfortable – sort of respecting their dignity – that's what I came into nursing for.
>
> (PROFKNOW Field notes 2004)

This testimony would, I think, be recognised by generations of nurses: it is part of the caring professional. The source of vocation, which has underpinned their commitment and their lifework, is nursing. So how do the reforms react to this precious ecology of commitment? One nurse describes her response to health reforms focusing on performativity:

My whole life is nursing: my whole sense of purpose is flattened by the web of bureaucratic bullshit in which I find myself. Instead of being at the bedside caring for patients, talking to patients, watching and observing them carefully; instead of working as a team of nurses who have these skills and build a community of caring, I end up doing other stuff altogether.

If you watched me, you'd be amazed, bloody amazed. A lot of the time now, I don't go anywhere near a bed, let alone a patient. What am I doing? I am sitting alone in front of a computer – filling in forms, compiling data, fiddling about with figures – actually fiddling is the word [laughs and laughs]. But really, is this what I'm here for – a young woman in the prime of life? I reckon I have so much to offer in terms of love and compassion for those people in need and I can't get near them. It makes me sick: still, at least I'll fit in here if I become sick!

(Ibid.)

These views about the effect of performance criteria-based reforms on these young nurses were shared by all the women I talked to. Perhaps the most powerful confirmation came from a much older nurse:

The job has changed so much and I and my friends (we're all about the same age, I guess around 50) ... we try to hold on to our old world in the face of these silly targets and tables. In my ward we still put the patient first, and we continue as a team of dedicated, experienced nurses to do this. It means we skimp on the paperwork, fill in the minimum, skip as many sections as we can. We sometimes get ticked off by the managers, and so on, but they know us and nothing ever happens. But it's a funny world where you have to make excuses for being a proper nurse – I sometimes wonder what is going on. Do they really want the NHS (National Health Service) to succeed, or something else?

(Ibid.)

These nurses were both in the same hospital and I was able to spend a day observing them at work. In the past 20 years, I have spent a good deal of my time observing professionals at work. So it was fascinating to see that the differences they had talked about really did exist in this practice.

An incidental realisation came when I negotiated entry. The nurses preferred that I came in a personal capacity, rather than as an official visitor. This is because of what Frank Furudi calls the 'culture of fear', which prevails in many professional workplaces, because of the obsessive micro-management of public services. Hence the nurses, even the experienced older ones, preferred that I kept them anonymous, and our meetings and my observations almost seemed covert at times.

My day in the hospital fully confirmed the different visions that the two cohorts of nurses presented. The younger nurses' wards were often empty of nursing carers, and patients lay alone. For long periods of the day, I found that the nurses congregated in a long back room, entering data into their computers. Occasionally, one or two would pop into the wards, often in response to a bleeper. But the clear centre of gravity of their professional life was the computer room. The difference, as I present it, seems almost too stark and polarised to be believable, but this was exactly how it was on these wards. In the older nurses' wards, a far more traditional pattern existed: nurses talking to patients, arranging beds, interacting with visitors and coping with emergency medical situations. But, above all, they were present in the ward and in the intimate caring relationship with their patients. The younger nurses' ward was simply far less hands-on; there was less of a presence throughout the day. Visits were occasional and felt minimal. They seemed to be dealing with clients, rather than servicing their patients, and we have seen when they described their nursing that this led to a strong sense of frustration. They had ended up in a very different relationship with those they were hoping to care for than they had envisaged.

One nurse who was willing to talk about these changes and go public with her views was Bernadette Murphy, a 38-year-old community staff nurse from Sutton in London. She said:

> Nursing is struggling to recruit people now because women's attitudes have changed so much. When I started my training in 1984, women weren't expected to go out and have a career. Today, nearly all my friends work. It's not surprising that people don't want to come into a profession like nursing when there are so many other more glamorous and better-paid careers out there.
>
> It is possible to earn a quite decent living from nursing, but to do so you have to really strive to get up the career ladder. And then that leaves you in a situation whereby you are no longer having that one-on-one contact with the patients, which is why you came into the profession in the first place. You get stuck doing administration and mountains of paperwork.
>
> (Doward and Reilly 2003: 7)

These nurses' commentaries on the effects of public service are similar to those of teachers, and to reports from a wide range of agencies and professional workers. There is also the question raised by one of them about just what the reforms are really about if they are so manifestly counterproductive. The nurse who raises the question 'do they really want the National Health Service to succeed?' is following a line pursued by other professionals. The 'culture of fear' and of 'blaming and shaming' under-performing hospitals through league tables and performance indicators is a strange strategy to employ. If it were so successful, why don't the much-emulated business management regimes employ such regulatory frameworks? In business, as we have said, the emphasis seems to be more on 'free markets', free action and deregulation. Indeed, the promise is held out that the high-performing hospitals will themselves be freed from micro-management and obsessive regulation. We face here a conundrum that is plainly baffling, not only to the workers but also to the professional elites in the health service. Again they are beginning to wonder, like the nurse: 'do they really want the National Health Service to succeed', or 'would some in government prefer a handover of this public service to private agencies, as has happened in so many other cases, such as the railways?'

In a recent study of NHS nurses, the levels of disenchantment and dysfunction were clearly evident. Kim Catcheside found that patterns of professionalism were being transformed by the reforms. She states of the NHS:

> Modern nurses are a health hazard, the old-fashioned TLC-trained ['tender loving care' – a summariser for a caring professional vocation] ones have all retired or resigned and the new lot, badly trained and poorly motivated, could not care less and are as likely in their ignorance to kill as to cure.
>
> (Arnold 2001: 12)

Behind this dysfunctionality, produced above all by the reforms, a growing body of opinion is emerging and calling into question the rationale of these reform initiatives. Professional leaders in the august and moderate body, the British Medical Association, have stated that the government reforms are 'changing the character of the NHS by turning it from an organisation that treats patients into a purchase of services provided by private contractors' (Carvel 2003: 2). Here, there are echoes of the frontline concerns expressed by nurses who see a changed relationship to patients being inflicted upon them, to the detriment of both the carers and the cared-for.

Mr James Johnson, chairman of the British Medical Association, said that the first sign of the government's long-term plans for the health service was the proposal to transfer 250,000 operations from the National Health Service to 'private treatment centres run by multi-national health corporations'. These transfer deals were worth £2 billion. Johnson argued that it was 'inevitable' that the centres would perform the simplest operations on the fittest patients, leaving more complex work to the NHS. This is, in fact, a remarkable echo of the private schools that take the best-equipped students, teach them with better facilities and higher teacher–pupil ratios, and then conspire with the user to pronounce that state schools are failing. Johnson, therefore, concludes that these changes in the health service are bound to lead to accusations that the cost of an NHS operation was greater. In a very insightful comment, he states that 'it is almost as if the NHS is being set up to fail' (ibid.).

The response of the young nurses to health reforms has been dramatically repeated by young teachers, who have spoken out against education reforms. Many teachers reiterate the same litany of complaints. One such teacher, Carmel Fitzsimons, qualified successfully but decided, after watching the reforms in action during her training year, that she could not face becoming a teacher. Her sense of mission and dedication was to a view of teaching as a creative and compassionate caring profession – the vision, in fact, of generations of women (and men) who have entered the teaching profession. These people have had an overriding sense of 'vocation' that has allowed them to tolerate low pay and low status for the sake of their 'dream' of contributing to society and to students' lives. The reforms do unimaginable damage to these high hopes and vivid visions.

In the event, Carmel determined not to follow her dream of going into teaching. She went further, writing an article on why – 'I Quit' (Fitzsimons 2001) – for one of the leading education newspapers in Britain. It was a very public and extremely articulate protest. What is interesting is her vision that teaching of the sort she wanted to practise should be a creative, innovative, intellectually invigorating profession. In this sense, she represents precisely the vanguard of creative and adventurous professionals that could carry teaching forward in these challenging times. As I shall argue later, this vanguard is a crucial element in the revitalisation of any profession, so the loss of such a bright young woman is of more than singular significance.

Jim Roberts is a teacher in his early forties, who works in a comprehensive school in Sussex, on the south coast of England. I have spent a good deal of time interviewing him, and indeed just talking to him, over the past year. He is known as a highly gifted teacher, a master of his craft. He is bright (has a PhD in Education) and ambitious. In short, he is just the kind of teacher to make up the 'vanguard' of a caring profession – aiming to deliver high standards of education.

Early on in our talks, he admits that his teaching work 'is his life'. In his early years in the 1980s and early 1990s, he was very close to the pupils he taught:

> JIM: I got to know them; got to know their parents; just fitted into that community really and absolutely loved it. Basically, I did everything I could and it didn't seem like work – it felt more like I looked forward to being in the community really – and then things started to change.

He continues,

> JIM: that whilst there was a degree of openness in the late eighties and early nineties, now the landscape is more sinister in my view.

I ask what he means. At first he talks about his own physical response:

> JIM: Fatigue comes to mind; initiative after initiative … that is so hard to actually name. I had sleepless nights over this because I was so intensely angry.

The general echoes of change, 'cascading from the centre' without consultation, had worn him down:

> JIM: I've been a bit down on it really because, you know, I came to the conclusion that all I was doing was supporting the system I was trying to challenge, or subvert it. You end up in a mode of support for it. I don't mean that I've been turned into someone who can't think for themselves, who can't step outside, who can't find alternatives, but the fact that I'm working within that context and for that group of people that are aiming to do this work is ultimately self-defeating because it's too powerful. It's got a singular mind; it's got a singular view … what many people describe as technical rationalism. How can we measure it,

how can we implement it? There is a disregard for teachers, as far as I can tell, and obviously I've looked at the face of it and I've seen disregard for teachers, disregard for – not kids, because they think they're doing it on behalf of the kids; they think they're doing it on behalf of the 'client'. (We are supposed to be calling them clients at these meetings, which I find abhorrent.) And so this whole thing about marketisation of education is staring me in the face and no matter what I say or what I do, or which group I work with, all we can keep doing is articulating that voice, which stands up against markets....

This sense of depression and demoralisation has progressively undermined Jim's sense of his professionalism; his sense of his life mission. Above all, he has watched how other colleagues have been treated (or mistreated) and how they have reacted. At times, he is moved to tears by what he says in the following section from one of our interviews:

JIM: It's the casualties along the way that get you down. It's the faces of the people that you've worked with who just can't take it any more. It's the stories of illness, the stories of people leaving the profession who are good – it's not people that you would think would leave. It's the stories of people in my own department, my colleagues who want to find an alternative way to live their lives. For example, I've only been at my new place – this is my third year – and a colleague who's a sculptor was really down on the school. He was down on the initiatives, he was down on the reforms, he was down on performance management. In my first meeting with him, we sat down and I asked him: 'What objectives are you setting?' He goes, 'Jim, I don't want to do this any more, I don't want to set objectives, I don't want to do performance management and I don't work here next September, so the school can stick it'.

INTERVIEWER: What age is he?

JIM: He's over 40 – 43, 44. I said, 'Phil, I'm with you mate, one hundred per cent behind you on this. If you're going to be here, what are we going to do? Can we look at this idea that you're an Arts Educator in residence?' All this stuff about 'let's get a so-called "artist-in-residence"'. Well, we discussed the possibility that we could suspend his timetable for a while and he could be ... along with his sort of career as an artist, he could have some time as an artist-in-residence in the timetable. And I put it to the Head and she said, 'I'm interested, I want these ideas. How much is it going to cost me? What's the effect on the staff going to be? How's it going to appear to them? How are we going to present it if we go through with it?' And so we worked on it, and we worked on it, and she was for it – she's a great woman in many ways: she has got humanistic values at the end of the day. So I basically had a package to offer him which I hoped would re-energise him, and he decided to go part-time and he, you know, I mean he was really grateful for the work that we put into getting this together.

INTERVIEWER: But, basically, he's pulled out?

JIM: Basically, he's put one foot out. He's now doing three days a week. Basically, what he's doing – he looks at the week like this – two days on, two days off, two days on, because he works through the weekend on his own. He's got a workshop that's just been built. He's had three exhibitions; he's now working in Lewes and he's full of the joy of being an artist.

INTERVIEWER: What does that look like to you? How does that …?

JIM: I'm pretty jealous, because I see someone who's now finding his feet again; who is doing, in a way, a better job in the classroom because he's happier within himself, and he's engaging with people outside who enjoy looking at his artwork and enjoy planning with him. He's looking at next year already to get his next exhibition now … it's not sorted out; he's doing little publications for his own work. Now, you know, it's not the kind of work that I do, but I've talked to you and you've talked to me about the kind of work I would like to do, so … but I see that he's found something that he wants to do and he can do it. He's running life-drawing classes on Fridays … When I left here tonight, he was running a life-drawing class which he could not be bothered to do two years ago because he was just burnt out – you know, he'd just had enough of it all, he wanted to get home, be with his wife.

INTERVIEWER: And what has happened there, what sorts of freedoms have re-energised him? And what has he escaped from? What has changed him?

JIM: What he feels like is that he's into the part-time culture, because the part-time culture is very different. He doesn't have a tutor group; he doesn't have to pass stupid bits of paper around all morning. His responsibilities have changed. He's not now expected to pass other bits of paper around which tell us what our benchmarks and targets should be for our Year 10 classes.

In reflecting on 'escape stories' like this one from a close friend, Jim also finds himself reluctantly, very reluctantly, questioning his own capacity to continue: 'I mean, I'm going home and I'm thinking, can I carry on like this? Can I do this any more?' Jim seems to be moving, much against his own expectations, towards a decision; a hugely emotional decision and one which, towards the end of our long sequence of talks, I really push him hard to confront: 'I've come to that decision. I don't like working in that school any more. I don't like working in a secondary school.'

INTERVIEWER: Because?

JIM: Because I get really upset. I get really upset by good teachers leaving – you know? … I see people destroyed. You know … [pause, clearly emotional].

INTERVIEWER: I know, it's an emotional thing …

JIM: Yeah.

INTERVIEWER: I mean, if it ...? Who else have you seen being destroyed, I mean ...?

JIM: Long-term illnesses. People coming back, trying to cope; crying in the morning because they can't do a cover lesson (which probably wouldn't bother them on another day) because they've got so much work to do ... People fighting with each other that wouldn't fight normally. Teachers taking it out on each other. Teachers taking it out on kids. Kids being unhappy because the curriculum doesn't speak to them.

INTERVIEWER: Can we ... I mean, the question that comes to mind there, Jim, is whether this is endemic to teaching, which is a stressful up-front profession, or the extent to which these teachers (are) being destroyed – which makes you tearful as we talk – is a result of the new conditions of change and reform? That's the question I'm trying ...

JIM: It's alienation. It's a divorce; they're divorced from what matters. Because the things that are being cascaded down ... don't really matter to them – they don't own them, they don't make them, they don't have a role in creating them or adapting them.

INTERVIEWER: But is it that that's destroying them?

JIM: It's that ... Yeah, it is that. Connected to and part of the reconstruction of the teacher – the notion that the teacher is being re-made through target setting; objectives; looking at performance management – that is a shambles, an absolute shambles! Teachers cannot cope with it as they don't own it, they don't know what it's about, they know it's just another form of appraisal. The management team in the school can't manage it because they don't understand it! They don't understand ...

In the end, I find Jim caught between this sense of impending crisis and desperation and a continuing sense of hope. He himself is suffering the same physical symptoms that he has seen so many others confront. This, remember, is a young, fit man full of professional wisdom, experience and compassion. A person who could offer so much in a wisely administered system of public education.

JIM: I think it's getting to the point where my health won't hold out. If I do what I'm doing, at the pace I'm doing it now, with the health problems I've had in the last couple of years – and I was fit and strong – I mean, don't forget I was telling you that I worked at the school every night; I played table tennis in a league with some of the students, and I was at school the next day bright as a button.

INTERVIEWER: And now?

JIM: And now really, at times, with the migraines, with the sickness, with the stomach ailments, with the anxiety; keeping up with the bureaucracy and keeping ahead of it in many ways, so that it doesn't beat you or it doesn't get you colonised, you know, it's taking its toll, and if I carry on the way I'm going, I don't think I can make it for another twenty years.

At the end of the last interview, Jim tries to summarise his feelings of frustration and enduring hope in the face of ill-conceived reforms and centrally prescribed initiatives, which transform his worthy contributions and undercut his professional mission. I ask him, does he have any concluding comment? He replies, 'I think I've cried enough now – I didn't realise that I was going to get so emotional!'

> INTERVIEWER: It's interesting, isn't it?
> JIM: Yeah.
> INTERVIEWER: Why do you think that is?
> JIM: Because when you're reflecting in a room like this, with someone I can get on with, I see the faces and I can't kind of tell you all the stories, but I can picture the hurt and anger, and the anxiety and the pressure and the frustration. And that's not just the teachers; it's coming out in the way the kids behave to each other and to us, you know? And we've got to fight, mate! We've got to keep the fight going, because it's just crap!

Even now, Jim knows what a noble calling teaching could be and why he so much wants to endure; to outlast the mindless machine of targets, tests and tables and to live to fight another day.

> There is a purpose to education, which I don't want to see destroyed. There are some fantastic teachers, some fantastic students who do fantastic work and I want them to have choice, mission, opportunity, social mobility and a sense of participating in their community – a sense that they own the culture of this land. And it has given my life meaning, if you take an existentialist point of view on it. We find and create meaning for our lives, and education is hope.

References

Arnold, S. (2001) 'Savage angels', *Observer Review*, 4 February.

Carvel, J. (2003) 'BMA warns of future of NHS', *The Guardian*, 10 October.

Doward, J. and Reilly, T. (2003) 'Shameful pay makes British women worst off in Europe', *The Observer*, 12 October.

Fitzsimons, C. (2001) 'I Quit', *Guardian Education*, 9 January.

PROFKNOW (2002–8) 'Professional Knowledge in Education and Health (PROFKNOW): restructuring work and life between state and citizens in Europe', UK: University of Brighton, Sweden: University of Gothenburg, Greece: National and Kopodistorian University of Athens, Finland: University of Joensuu, Spain: University of Barcelona, Portugal: University of the Azores, Ireland: St Patrick's College, Dublin City University, Sweden: University of Stockholm. Available at: www.ips.gu.se/english/Research/ research_programmes/pop/current_research/profknow/ (accessed 6 September 2013).

Part III

8 All the lonely people

The struggle for private meaning and public purpose in education

How do you constantly innovate in a society that is already affluent? By creating needs, that's how. By making people feel lonely and anxious and inadequate.

(Leith 2006)

The long-term effect of US culture as it spreads to every nook and cranny in every desert and every mountain valley will be the end of mankind. Our extraordinary greed for material possessions, the way we go about nurturing that greed, the lack of balance in our lives, and our cultural arrogance will kill us off within a century unless we learn to stop and think.

(Thesiger 2002)

Introduction

In the period since 1989, we have witnessed the emergence of a 'New World Order'. Alongside this, a range of commentating intellectuals have argued that we are at the 'end of history', where the 'one best system' will set the economic and social pattern for the whole globe.

Yet increasingly, this complacent view of triumph and culminating victory has been challenged. These challenges preceded the terrible events of 11 September 2001 in Manhattan. As Michael Ignatieff has argued:

The essential problem is that the victors of the Cold War now run a global world order that has no perceived legitimacy among billions of human beings, especially in the Islamic world.

(Ignatieff 2001: 4)

This chapter is not about the war of civilisation that might ensue between the Western Christian and the Islamic worlds. It is about another legitimacy crisis altogether – one within the Western world itself – and it is concerned to show how this impinges on the world of education and teacher professionalism.

For the past five years – with each new research project I have been involved in – I have noted a change, a dramatic change, in the way that people talk about their lives. Much of my research work is 'life history' work: the detailed historical study of people's life stories in occupational settings. As Levinson (1979), Levinson and Levinson (1996) and Sheehy (1998) have evidenced, many people define their life around a central 'dream' or mission, or an ideal that they want to attain. This ideal might range from the modest to the heroic, but it is a central heartland in the way that life stories are told and people often judge the 'success' or 'failure' of their lives against this yardstick. Having 'dreams', or 'pet projects' or 'missions', has provided strategic guidance in the business of making a life and leading a purposeful and meaningful life.

Without these 'dreams', it would seem, life might become mundane, episodic, unfocused, shapeless and without any overriding meaning or energising passion. One distraction of their life 'missions' would be more than a change from modernist myth to post-modern *bricolage*: it would represent the erosion of long-established modes of 'making a life'.

For the past 30 years, I have conducted social research in a variety of educational and policy settings. Most commonly, my work has focused on public services – notably in education, but also in medicine, the police and the social services. I have, if you will, become familiar with the 'ecology' of public services; with the way in which people conduct their professional lives and generate, thereby, professional and personal meanings and missions.

Much of my recent work has focused on the life histories and work histories of professional people (Goodson 2004; Goodson 2005). In this work, there is a chance to confront, in great personal detail, how people manage their lives. Above all, you see how people's sense of purpose and meaning is played out in their workplaces and their own personal 'hinterlands'. In some ways, I often think that this work is similar to that of wildlife experts studying the changing ecology and habitat of a particular species. Over time, such studies provide the researcher with a finely grounded sense of whether dramatic change is underway. In wildlife studies, global warming is generating such dramatic change at the moment.

Studies of professional life and work are beginning to provide similar snapshots of dramatic change. For the past five years, together with Andy Hargreaves, I have been directing a large research team, which is funded by the Spencer Foundation to look at 'change over time' in American and Canadian schools. I spent six months each year in America conducting this research. For the other six months, I examined similar data in the United Kingdom and Europe.

The research was set up to explore change in schools over a 30–40-year period. To do this, we interviewed cohorts of teachers from the 1950s and 1960s (Cohort 1); the 1970s and 1980s (Cohort 2); and the 1990s through to the present (Cohort 3). These interviews focused on the detailed life histories and work histories of the teachers and hence provide a snapshot of professional life and work in the education setting.

Most research has its epiphanic moments – if you are lucky. For me, it was trying out some interview schedules with Cohort 3 teachers. We had added a final question: 'Are there any projects or interests outside your work that you would like to tell us about?' Cohort 1 and 2 teachers had spoken about their teaching as a central project, often as a 'passion'. Teaching, for many (though, of course, by no means all) was their 'life work' and a source of enduring passion and commitment. Teaching gave their life personal meaning within a collective project or vocation that expressed deeply held values and beliefs. In their professional life, then, personal meanings and public purposes were held in a balance that provided some sense of purposeful life work.

For Cohort 3 teachers answering my question, this sense of purpose had patently collapsed. In the early stages of the interview, they proffered the opinion that teaching was 'just a job'; 'only a pay cheque'; 'I turn up and do what I'm told between 8 and 5'; 'I follow the rules'. Their strategy was one of minimal engagement and teaching was far from being 'purposeful life work'. My epiphany came when they talked about 'other interests or projects'. Here, the change in body language was marked: they leaned forward in their seats, their eyes shone and their hand movements were animated. 'Did they have other interests?' 'Oh yes, I'm planning to get out in the next two years and start a beauty clinic … I'm so excited'; 'I'm training in the evenings to become an occupational therapist, I can't wait to begin my new life'; 'I'm saving up to retire at 50 – it's only five years away … then my life will begin.'

For these professionals, it would seem that the workplace and its meaning are dramatically different from the experience of previous generations, but perhaps teaching is an exception. Other research, however, points to a similar phenomenon: a growing range of studies point to a crisis of personal meaning and collective, public purpose at the heart of Western life. These confirm my belief that the 'New World Order' is in profound danger of losing its legitimacy and indeed credibility with its own citizens, certainly in the struggle to deliver better public services and a reinvigorated public life.

Richard Sennett speaks of his own epiphany at the Swiss mountain resort of Davos where, for the past few years, he has attended a winter meeting of elite business and political leaders. The World Economic Forum at Davos 'runs more like a court than a conference. Its monarchs are the heads of big banks or international corporations' (Sennett 1999: 66). However, Sennett finds a dilemma at the heart of the proceedings, namely that the regime is 'losing the battle for the hearts and minds' of ordinary people. In a peculiar and deeply disheartening way, it is almost a rerun of the way that the defeated Communist regimes first lost the engagement and commitment of their own people before losing the global battle. Sennett comments:

> It therefore seemed to me, as I wandered in and out of the conference halls, weaved through the tangle of limousines and police, or the mountainous village streets, that this regime might at least lose its current hold over the imaginations and sentiments of those down below.
>
> (Sennett 1999: 147)

Sennett argues that, having studied new social and workplace patterns:

> One of the unintended consequences of modern capitalism is that it has strengthened the value of place, arousing a longing for community. All the emotional conditions we have explored in the workplace animate that desire;

the uncertainties of flexibility; the absence of deeply rooted trust and commitment; the superficiality of teamwork; but most of all, the spectre of failing to make something of oneself in the world, 'to get a life' through one's work. All these conditions impel people to look for some other scene of attachment and depth.

(Ibid.: 138)

What we may be seeing, then, is the beginning of a substantial 'turning away' from one of the major sites of collective purpose and social engagement – the public service workplace. The other side of this movement is a 'turning towards' the individual; the personal; the consumable; the special interest; the private purpose. It is not quite as stark as 'there is no such thing as society' or that 'greed is good', but it is a growing focus on the private world of the individual self.

In a general sense, it is a turn away from common pursuits and public purpose towards personal missions and private consumption. This kind of turning away from the public and common purpose is often seen in societies that lack a legitimate moral mission. For instance, in South Africa, during the period of apartheid:

> Many white bystanders who intellectually opposed apartheid adopted a passive opposition. They retreated into private life, cut themselves off from the news media, refused to talk politics with friends, and adopted an intense immersion in private diversions such as sport, holidays and families.

(Marshall 2001: 9)

In his remarkable study of American life, Robert Putnam has documented a similar kind of atrophying of American public purpose. He contrasts the baby boomer generation, who emerged as a social and political force in the 1960s, with the contemporary 'Generation X'ers':

> Unlike boomers, who were once engaged, X'ers have never made the connection to politics, so they emphasise the personal and private over the public and collective. Moreover, they are visually oriented, perpetual surfers, multi-taskers, interactive media specialists. In both personal and national terms, this generation is shaped by uncertainty (especially given the slow growth, inflation-prone 1970s and 1980s), insecurity (for these are the children of the divorce explosion), and an absence of collective success stories – no victorious D-Day and triumph over Hitler, no exhilarating, liberating marches on Washington and triumph over racism and war, indeed hardly any 'great collective events' at all. For understandable reasons, this cohort is very inwardly focussed.

(Putnam 2001: 259)

Putnam shows how, at every level in American life, social activities and public purposes are in dramatic decline. To employ the previous analogy with wildlife, the 'global warming' of globalisation is destroying the social ecology at a dramatic and unprecedented rate. The changes have come within one generation – an incredibly short time span in human history.

> Middle-aged and older people are more active in organisation than younger people, attend church more often, vote more regularly, both read and watch the news more frequently, are less misanthropic and more philanthropic, are most interested in politics, work on more community projects, and volunteer more.
>
> (Ibid.: 247–8)

Putnam notes the change effects; the range of passions, purposes and meanings:

> Not all social networks have atrophied. Thin, single-stranded, surf-by interactions are gradually replacing dense, multi-stranded, well-exercised bonds. More of our social connectedness is one-shot, special purpose and self-oriented. As sociologist Morris Janowitz foresaw several decades ago, we have developed 'communities of limited liability' or what sociologists Claude Fischer, Robert Jackson and their colleagues describe more hopefully as personal communities. Large groups with local chapters, long histories, multiple objectives, and adverse organisations are being replaced by more evanescent, single-purpose organisations.
>
> (Ibid.: 183–4)

These changes reflect a transformation in our social and political purposes, and in the vehicles we have traditionally used to carry those purposes. It is, as with global warming and wildlife, a destruction of unprecedented speed and range. But since the implications drive into the heartland of personal meaning, mission and motivation, we have not yet witnessed what this may mean for the human species and the nature of human beings. It is likely to transform our understandings and our somewhat stabilised view since the Enlightenment, of what it is to be a human being. In doing so, it will revolutionise our core concepts, such as what constitutes 'a life' and 'a career', besides having similarly potent effects on other concepts like 'love', 'commitment', 'community', 'democracy', 'society' – even 'God'. The reasons for this social revolution can be traced back to similar origins to the causes of global warming:

> In the 1980s and 1990s, deregulation of government functions and services was the rage. In less than twenty years, the global marketplace successfully absorbed large parts of what formerly was the government sphere – including mass transportation, utilities and telecommunications – into the commercial realm. Now the economy has turned its attention to the last remaining independent sphere of human activity: the culture itself, cultural rituals, community events, social gatherings, the arts, sports and games, social movements, and civic engagements are all being encroached upon by the commercial sphere.
>
> (Rifkin 2001: 10)

Jeremy Rifkin concludes:

> The great issue in the coming years is whether civilisation can survive with
> a greatly reduced government and cultural sphere and where only the com-
> mercial sphere is left as the primary mediator of human life.

> (Ibid.)

One of the major questions for social scientists is where should we look for
answers to Rifkin's question. If we study human ecology, as we might study
wildlife ecology, the signs seem alarmingly clear. Human life is being transformed at an astonishingly rapid speed; established social and community bonds
and purposes are dissolving. Alongside this, the meanings of work, career, love,
commitment and overall purpose are subject to seismic change, so that the very
understanding of what has been thought of as 'a human being' for the past two
or more centuries may be undergoing transformation.

One driving force in this revolution is the commercialisation and, in that most
apt of phrases, the 'privatisation' of much of our social and community life. Up
until now, at the social and public level, we have tended to operate 'mixed economies', where the private and commercial were set within nation-states against
public sectors and services. This might be seen as providing healthy 'checks and
balances' on the headlong commercialisation of all public life. Since 1980, with
deregulation, these 'checks and balances' in social and political life have been
progressively eradicated so that 'social democratic' politics itself, along with its
pursuit of social justice, seems to be going the way of the dinosaur.

The analogy with natural evolution, though, is a dangerous one, as has often
been pointed out. For humankind and human life is distinguished from animal
life by its command of language and thought, and by its delicate fabric of human
purpose and meaning-making. For a new era to be launched, which attacks long-
established hinterlands of human meaning, passion and purpose, it is at the very
least a dangerous enterprise and at worst an apocalyptic scenario. For this enterprise to be attempted, at one and the same time as social critique and commentary are narrowed and utilitarianised, seems a form of arrogant triumphalism,
with huge risks attached.

We are entering a new era in human history associated with transforming technology and globalisation; this much is incontestable. What is more contestable is
whether all the 'checks and balances' I have referred to should be thrown away;
whether culture and thought should be commercialised. Traditionally, when
dictatorships suppress all critique, they ossify and ultimately fail. The defence of
'checks and balances' of culture might therefore be a smart move for the very
forces currently planning their takeover.

But how can we judge these and other questions? Where can the social scientist look for answers? In this chapter, I have chosen to search for answers in the
very fields that Rifkin argues are ripe for commercialisation – the fields of culture, education and public services. I believe this is the right place to look,
because it is here that commercial takeover may become commercial 'overreach'.
Because here, the places where we socialise our young, discuss issues of morality

and purpose, implant long-cherished ideals of patriotism and citizenship and provide public goods and public services, are being subjected to colossal change.

These, then, are the places I shall look at, but how will one judge? What will comprise our evidence? Most importantly, we shall try to search for the sources of human meaning; the way that people talk about their lives, manage their lives and pursue dreams and purposes in their lives. This must always comprise the moral centre of a society, its sources of ongoing legitimacy. For if the overall systems and activities of a society become uncoupled from the collective and individual purposes of the people that comprise that society, you have a classic 'legitimisation crisis', a situation where the demands and ongoing aspirations of the system are divorced or opposed to the collective and personal purposes and passions of the people. By focusing on life and work interviews, our studies will try to examine the relationship between new commercialising and privatising initiatives, and the sense of meaning and purpose that has characterised human life since the Enlightenment.

Throughout, our focus will be on what motivates people and sponsors their meaning-making, and we shall see what role the acquisition of goods and money plays in that process. At root, we shall explore whether commercialisation and privatisation should become our sole routes to human meaning, and whether this overarching project is winning 'hearts and minds', as people construct their life narratives. Our focus, then, will be on the projects and 'dreams' that people construct and explore as they go about living their lives, but here I shall look specifically at how attempts to commercialise the public services through the introduction of targets and tests affect people's sense of meaning and mission.

Personal missions and professional development

I referred earlier to the five-year Spencer Foundation study, and it is from this research study that I shall derive much of my data for the next section. Our research took place at a time of very rapid restructuring in US and Canadian schooling.

Many current school reforms and change theories start from the assumption that since all is not well with the schools (true), reform and change can only help the situation (false). The assumption is held that the clear enunciation of objectives, backed by a battery of tests, accompanied by accountability strategies and confirmed by a range of financial incentives and payments by results, will inevitably raise school standards. The teacher is positioned as a key part of this delivery system, but it is the technical aspects of teacher professionalism that are stressed, rather than the 'professional biography' – the personal missions and commitments that underpin the teacher's sense of vocation and caring professionalism.

We can overstress this growing technical element, which is far from universal, and we can overstate the attack on the teacher's sense of vocation. Nonetheless, what is irrefutable is that there has been little work on the 'personality of change'. In very few instances have school reforms or change theories been promulgated that place personal development and change as central 'building blocks' in the process. Instead, changes have been pursued in ways that seem to insist this will happen, *in spite* of the teacher's personal beliefs and missions. All too often, the 'personality of change' has been seen as the 'stumbling block' of real reform, rather than as a crucial 'building block'.

In this section, I want to evidence why such a view is potentially catastrophic for the current wave of reforms and change initiatives. Before I do this, however, let us examine a common myth in current school restructuring. It has a number of different embodiments, but goes something like this: in the old days (the 1960s and 1970s), in many Western countries, we operated loosely organised, democratic social services and welfare states. Because the economies were affluent, discipline was fairly casual and school teachers (like other professionals) were allowed uncommon degrees of autonomy and professional self-direction. The result was a weak sense of social discipline and low school standards.

Now those days are over, governments are firmly in control of the schools – objectives and tests are being clearly defined, and school standards and discipline will steadily improve.

With regard to the teachers, the story goes this way: the old days of teachers as autonomous and self-directed professionals are over; the 'new professional' is technically competent, complies with new guidelines and ordinances and views teaching as a job where, like others, he/she is managed and directed and delivers what is asked of him/her. Educational change at the level of teaching means replacing, as soon as possible, the 'old professionals' with the 'new professionals'. Once this task is completed and the 'old professionals' have been 'mopped up', a new, more efficient and improved schooling system will emerge.

In some ways, this story is similar to the restructuring initiatives pursued in a range of industries and services, but I want to suggest that, in education in particular, it is proving a dangerous package to pursue. Let us look at this from the perspective of teachers. From the point of view of the 'old professionals', the pattern is clear: 'the game is up', they are told. Either they abandon their dreams of professional autonomy or they take early retirement. The results have been predictable everywhere – a huge rush of 'early retirements', alongside a group of teachers who 'hang in' in a state of despair and disenchantment.

For the reformers, this might be deemed a small transitional price to pay for replacing the 'old professionals' with 'new delivery-conscious professionals'. But there we must stop. Is it really that simple? Even in business, restructuring has proved more complex and contradictory than expected. In schools, the business is messily human and personal. Here, despair and disenchantment lead directly to uninspired teaching and spoilt student life-chances.

I want to suggest that such a perception amongst 'old professionals' is a much wider disaster for the complex ecology of schools. The term 'old professional' needs to be further elucidated. I do not mean this to imply a particular professional of a certain age and stage; rather, it means a view of teaching where the professionalism is expressed and experienced as more than just a job – it is seen as a caring vocation. At heart, it means viewing the work of teaching as comprising more than material reward and technical delivery, as a form of work overlaid with purpose, passion and meaning. This may sound too pious (for it is not always – not in all circumstances – as we all have bad days, bad periods), but it means a kind of professionalism where 'vocation' is part of the package, where 'ideals' are held and pursued. 'Old professional', then, captures an aspiration that is felt by both old and new teachers – it refers to a kind of professionalism and it is called 'old' because it was once more common and easier to pursue than it is in current circumstances.

In schools, the attack on 'old professional' vocationalism becomes a problem for a number of reasons:

- memory loss
- mentoring loss
- teacher retention and recruitment.

Let me take these in turn.

Memory loss

I have become very interested in what happens when the more mature members of an industry or community are given early retirement or subjected to change and reform that they disagree with, as is the case in so many of our schools. Interestingly, a range of new studies in Britain is looking at what happened to another delicate service industry – the railways. Tim Strangleman, a railway signalman himself, has been doing a PhD on the railway industry. He has been particularly interested in the occupational identity that railway workers have, and their skill and pride in 'running the railways' – a complex task with a wide range of skills and techniques learned on the job and passed on from worker to worker. The railways are being restructured and divided into separate, self-managing regional companies, each with their own budgets. The workers' skill and pride in their jobs has been a central ingredient in the old national service – a feature of old railway professionals, one might say. But now, with the restructuring, 'Any residual pride in the job is wearing thin as new managers, with no railway background themselves, foster the notion that 'it's just another job, like shelling peas' (Newnham 1997: 28).

This reflects a similar phrase used again and again by younger teachers in our studies, 'After all, teaching is only a job, like any other.' In his railway study, Strangleman also makes connections. For instance, he:

> makes a surprising comparison with the banking industry, where the term 'corporate memory loss' has been coined to describe the process whereby layers of unquantifiable knowledge, acquired through years of experience, were swept aside during the Eighties by an over-confident managerial class with no sense of the past. In the banking context, such tacit knowledge – 'rule of thumb, finger-in-the-air stuff' – might be the difference between sound and unsound investment. On the railways, it might be the difference between life and death.
>
> (Ibid.)

This was written in 1997. Since then, Britain has witnessed a number of horrendous railway accidents, culminating in the Hatfield crash, which led to the whole railway system being almost shut down for weeks.

The closure of Railtrack and its effective denationalisation has led to a series of reports and commentaries that begin to face the reality of what has happened. For example, Keith Harper talks about the fact that: 'during this period, many disenchanted senior railway staff started to leave Railtrack, to be replaced in key appointments by people with little knowledge of the industry' (Harper 2001: 10).

Likewise, Christopher Green, Chief Executive of Virgin Trains, has argued that 'the most important criticism of the railway is that it has lost "the art of delivery" '. He says that the industry had thrown away 'the Sergeant Major of the track', by which he means the 'dedicated railway man who daily used to inspect a ten-mile length of track and knew what was wrong'. These men, disillusioned and forgotten, have gradually left the industry. They have been replaced by 'clever technology', dismissed by Green as 'hardly out of university experimental stage which have thrown up projects without being thoroughly tested' (Green 2001: 28).

Strangely, however, the learning curve seems impossibly long for those civil servants responsible for this initiative. Sir Steve Robson is the former second permanent secretary at the Treasury; whilst he was in position he worked on several privatisations, including the railways and the private finance initiative. In his analysis of the problem, he shows absolutely no awareness that work and motivation and the 'personalities of change' are a central issue. Instead, he returns to the common diagnosis – that this is primarily a problem of money and financial incentives. In his conclusion to a recent piece, he argued:

> What about Railtrack? Where should we go now? The basic issue is the same – management and incentives. Rail infrastructure needs to be run by top quality managers who are incentivised, and empowered to do a good job. The issue for all of us who wish to see this country have a good rail system is whether the structure which comes out of administration will attract such managers and give them the right incentives and authority.
>
> (Robson 2001: 28)

The myopic absurdity of this diagnosis is breathtaking in the light of what has happened to the railways. It is as if the workforce and its inherited and ongoing expertise are of no importance in the delivery of the railway services. Again, government bodies return to the problem of how to incentivise the elite. This elite has been superannuated and incentivised to the most absurd level, and the result has been a catastrophic failure of delivery. One wonders what kind of experiences will be required for the learning curve in certain sectors of government to move upwards.

Perhaps, then, in school reform, the purging of the 'old professionals' in the face of new change and reform might be a similarly catastrophic move. All too clearly, attention to these aspects of the 'personality of change' is worth much greater attention.

Mentoring loss

Each school is a carefully constructed community: if the elders in that community feel disenchanted and undervalued, this is a problem for the community of the school. It then becomes a problem for the successful delivery of the educational services the school provides – in short, a problem of school performance and educational standards.

Robert Bly (1991) has written about the problems for any community when the 'elders' of that community are disenchanted, disorientated and disregarded. This problem is particularly relevant when considering teachers. Let me give a specific example of what is lost when a whole cohort or section of teachers responds in this way. In our studies, we have witnessed a number of schools where the sense of drift, of anarchy, of a lack of direction, is palpable. In one of the schools – an innovative, landmark school in Toronto founded in the 1960s – the ex-headmaster judged the problem to be exactly as with the railways.

The old cohort of founding professionals had become disenchanted by the new changes and reforms. As a result, they either took early retirement or remained at work in a disaffected and disengaged way. The problem this posed, according to the ex-headmaster, was that nobody therefore took on the mentoring of young teachers. They just arrived and went to work; it was just a job and they followed management instructions and state guidelines as best they could. As a result, the 'old professionals' (in this specific case, mainly the elders) kept their professional knowledge to themselves and the chain of professional transmission was broken – the 'layers of unquantifiable knowledge, acquired through years of experience' remained un-transmitted to the new generation of teachers. The school then suffered 'corporate memory loss'.

The result, apparently, was a school without passion or purpose; without direction. People turned up to do a job like any other job, without a sense of overriding vocation or ideals and, as soon as they could, went home to their other life where, presumably, their passion and purpose resided and revived.

Teacher retention and recruitment

In the first two sections, we have seen how 'old professional' vocationalism has declined in teaching, either formally through early retirement or spiritually because a wider cohort of teachers has become detached and disillusioned. At one stage, reform advocates and change theorists thought that this evacuation by 'old professionals' was a sign of the success of their strategy. As a result, they argued, schools would be rejuvenated and filled with eager advocates of the new reforms.

This has proved to be both wildly optimistic and misguided. The problem of retention (or the non-problem in the eyes of reformers) has quickly shifted to the problem of recruitment. This second trend is seen as a problem, because even the wildest change advocates recognise that schools have to be staffed!

What research is showing is that, in many ways, the problems of retention and recruitment are related and have the same root cause. It seems that many of the younger cohorts of would-be teachers are looking at the job and making similar judgements to their 'old professional' elders. The 'purging of the old' stands alongside the 'turning-off' of the young.

To sum up the reasons, this situation exists because, in Bob Hewitt's felicitous phrase, 'initiative and resourcefulness are banned' in teaching now, and, in his farewell article, 'I quit', he says:

> To see schools these days as filled just with bureaucratic bullshit is to seriously miss the point, however. Education has traditionally been about freedom. But there is no freedom any more. It's gone. Initiative and resourcefulness are banned. Every school has become a part of the gulag. How else could inspectors time the literacy hour with stopwatches, or a teacher be dismissed over a bit of missing paperwork?
>
> (Hewitt and Fitzsimons 2001: 3)

Whilst some younger recruits accept this form of occupational identity, far more are deciding to take their initiative and resourcefulness into occupations that value rather than denigrate these characteristics. For example, Carmel Fitzsimons has just qualified as a teacher, but sees no possibility of actually practising. In the article, 'I quit', she says:

> I don't think teachers are uncreative – but creativity is being crushed out of them by the grinding cogs of bureaucracy and filing.
>
> To give you a glimpse: for every lesson a teacher is supposed to prepare assessment sheets from the previous lesson; they must then reflect upon the issues the assessment throws up. Then they must prepare a lesson plan – based on long-term, medium-term and short-term objectives from the curriculum; and having delivered the lesson, they must write up an evaluation of how the lesson went and then individually assess the progression of each child's learning. This can mean five sheets of written paper per lesson for each of the five lessons a day. Add the individual record of each child, the reading records and the collection of money for the school trip and you start to wonder whether there is any time left for getting your coat on before legging it across the playground.
>
> (Ibid.: 2)

Alistair Ross and a team of researchers have been studying teacher recruitment and retention for the past three years. Their findings make salutary reading for the advocates of reform and change:

> We asked those who were leaving for other careers what it was that they saw as attractive in their new work.

Three-fifths of all teachers taking up work outside the profession do not find that teaching allows them to be creative and resourceful. These factors used to be one of the key defining elements of the teaching profession: people joined the profession because it used to offer them autonomy, creativity and the ability to use one's initiative.

What has happened to the profession that has caused these teachers, at least, to become so disillusioned that they seek alternative careers? This question, to teachers, is rhetorical. The ways in which teaching has become managed, has become 'accountable' and has been subjected to control and direction, have contributed to demotivation.

(Ross 2001: 9)

They also found that the problems of recruitment and retention were not primarily economic, as has so often been argued:

We have also found that for teachers leaving the profession, it isn't high alternative salaries that are attracting them out. Of our sample of teachers leaving for other careers, only 27 per cent would be earning more than they earned as teachers; 27 per cent said that they would earn the same as they had earned as in their previous teaching post; and 45 per cent were going to posts paying *less* than they had earned in their last teaching post. It is the change in the nature of teaching that is behind the crisis points we have described.

(Ibid.)

Conclusion: the paradox of performativity in education

Behind the question of the 'personality of change' stands the complex issue of what constitutes professional knowledge and action; what characterises teacher professionalism? In our book, *Teachers' Professional Lives* (Goodson and Hargreaves 1996), we defined five kinds of professionalism: classical, flexible, practical, extended and complex. We predicted that in the twenty-first century, a complex, post-modern professionalism would emerge, based on a range of characteristics – most notably 'the creation and recognition of high task "complexity", with levels of status and reward appropriate to such complexity' (1996: 21). We argued that this would lead to the emergence of a more personalised notion of professionalism, based upon 'a self-directed search and struggle for "continuous learning" related to one's own expertise and standards of practice, rather than compliance with the enervating obligations of "endless change" demanded by others' (ibid.).

Geoff Troman (1996) has examined the rise of what he calls the 'new professionals'. This group accepts the new political dispensation and hierarchies of the reform process, new governmental guidelines and national objectives and curriculum. However, some members of the group have taken aspects of the 'old professionals'' view of the world. The 'old professionals' believed in teachers' collective control of their work and in professional and personal autonomy. In some respects, the 'new professionals' have found a way to continue being semi-autonomous and, in this sense, are pioneering a new complex professionalism, which may moderate the bad effects of over-zealous reform initiatives.

But Troman was studying schools in the UK from the 1980s through to the 1990s – before the excesses of the reform process noted above began to bite. He argued that: 'The strategy of resistance within accommodation is possible, at this time, only because spaces exist within the work of teaching and management–teacher relations' (Troman 1996: 485).

In fact, recent reforms in a number of countries have sought to close these spaces for semi-autonomous personal and professional action. In doing so, they are tightening the screw too much and threatening to turn teaching into a profession that is attractive only to the compliant and docile, and conversely unattractive to the creative and resourceful. By pushing too far, they threaten to turn our schools into places of uniformity and barrenness – hardly sites on which standards will rise and educational inspiration will flourish.

One way to view these changes and reforms is through the clear signs that it is the most creative and resourceful of our teachers who are the most disenchanted with new prescriptions and guidelines. In a recent survey, teachers have generally listed 'government initiatives' as the major reason for their wish to leave teaching. It is instructive to view any profession or workforce not as a monolithic entity but as made up of a number of segments. Looking at the teaching profession, we might distinguish three segments:

- an elite or vanguard made up of the top 10 to 20 per cent;
- a mainstream 'backbone' group comprising 60 to 70 per cent; and
- a borderline group comprising 10 to 20 per cent.

The elite group are the most creative and motivated group and often help define, articulate and extend the 'mission of teaching' generally – and of a school in particular. Their commitment to change and reform is a basic prerequisite for successful implementation; their disenchantment and disengagement leave change and reform as hollow rhetoric. This is, not least, because of their mentorship and leadership of the mainstream group of teachers. This group, comprising 60 to 70 per cent of honest, hardworking professionals, makes up the backbone of the teaching profession. The interplay of mentorship and leadership between the elite and the backbone is reciprocal and vital in motivating and defining the teaching workforce. It is also central in the maintenance of a sense of vocation and mission.

The third group in any profession is the 10 or 20 per cent who are minimally involved: for this group, it is 'just a job' and some individuals border on incompetent. This group has been the focus of many of the reforms and accountability strategies articulated by Western governments recently, yet one senses that, like the poor, they are 'always with us'. By focusing the reforms on this group, little is actually changed with regard to their performance and motivation. However, and paradoxically, the world is transformed for the elite and the backbone. By attacking the small substandard groups, which all professions contain, many of the reforms have encountered a colossal downside by demotivating the vanguard and the backbone. Frankly, to use business jargon, the balance sheet's costs and benefits are deeply unsatisfactory – the benefits are minimal and the costs are colossal. If it were a simple question of financial bottom lines and profits, action would be taken immediately: the reforms would be aborted and new, more motivating and sensitive initiatives would be undertaken. However, since in education it is a question of human judgment and political face, one senses a long war of attrition before sensible judgements are made. In the meantime, the system continues its downward spiral.

The signs of disaffection grow daily: not just problems of teacher recruitment, but problems of student disaffection and recruitment, and the number of students being educated at home rather than at school continues to rocket under the National Curriculum in England. Meanwhile, in more vital and entrepreneurial environments like Hong Kong, the government is moving away from a rigid syllabus-defined, subject-centred curriculum to a loose facilitating framework of 'key learning areas'. Each school defines its own curriculum within that facilitating framework, and the teacher's personal and professional judgment is given greater provenance. Here, respect for the 'personality of change' is built in to encourage greater creativity and competitiveness.

Above all, the reforms return some personal and professional discretion to the teacher; to the 'layers of unquantifiable knowledge acquired through years of experience', which only a foolish management group sought to expunge in the schools (as in the railways). In the railways, the result of the over-zealous pursuit of reform was a death-dealing dysfunctional system. In the school, the effect on student life-chances will amount to the same thing.

Much of the organisational change pursued from the 1980s through to the early twenty-first century has been concerned with restructuring or replacing large, and sometimes inflexible, supply-side organisations with more flexible, market-focused and delivery-conscious organisations. This has been a period of rapid restructuring, conducted at a time of global reorganisation and huge technological transformation. Not surprisingly, then, many reforms pursued for the most defensible of reasons have turned out to have unpredictable results. Revolutionary organisational change always works with a downside – it was so in the Industrial Revolution and it is the same during this period of technological and global transformation. These unintended side-effects of change are slowly becoming visible as the first wave of transformation begins to slow down. Whether these side-effects serve to refract, reverse or abort the transformational changes will depend to some extent on our recognising their character and cause. In this chapter, I show that to ignore the unintended downsides of change will indeed threaten the momentum and ongoing success of restructuring and reform efforts.

Many reforms have common characteristics: they seek to articulate new visions and targets associated with accountability structures and standards. In the public services, the micro-management of these standards dominates reform efforts, and often achieves a level of detail and definition that is complex and sometimes infinitesimal. One paradox at the heart of the new 'free market' world order is that, whilst business is less and less regulated, the public sector becomes micro-managed at a level of minute mandate and detail.

Many of the reforms that have driven up productivity and profitability in the business sector have 'crossed over' into the public sector, but with the regulatory and micro-management characteristics noted above mixed alongside, this com-bination not unexpectedly produces some profoundly contradictory effects.

One characteristic of reforms in both business and the public sectors is that new initiatives aim to replace the existing 'regimes of truth', or 'vocabularies of motives' or 'mission statements' of the organisation-to-be-reformed. In this sense, organisational change involves the replacement, or indeed destruction, of one 'organisational memory' for a new memory. In business, the destruction of memory might be easily accommodated, but in the delicate ecology of social services this is often, as we shall see, a rather more perilous process. Services can break down and lives and life-chances can be lost in the turmoil.

The same juxtaposition works when considering the personal 'missions' that people bring to their employment. In business, new flexible regimes – especially in the IT area and a range of dot.com companies – often free up employees to pursue their own 'projects'. This is viewed as strengthening the innovative and delivery-driven mission of the company. In the micro-managed and re-regulated regimes of the public sector, the opposite is happening. Workers' missions and projects are being replaced by mandates that define standards and behaviour. Hence, any harmonisation between organisational missions and personal motives becomes accidental and haphazard at best, and confrontational and contradic-tory at worst. This can mean that people working in the restructured public services begin to take their hearts and minds from the enterprise and perform as technicians, carrying out the mandates and missions of others in minimalist fashion: 'it's just a job – I turn up and I do what I'm told'. This is a long way from the personally felt, caring professionalism that once characterised the top end of public sector provision.

The mention of a past 'caring professionalism' will immediately ring alarm bells for some (note that I specifically talk of the 'top end', the best of public sector provision). The claim, however, smacks of 'golden age' reminiscences of past harmony and smooth public sector provision. It was, of course, never like that – 'nostalgia ain't what it used to be'. Indeed, some public services developed a culture that favoured the service providers rather than the clients and, at times, trade union action exacerbated this problem. The issue of 'for whose benefit is the public sector run?' is a perennial problem – public and professional groups can hijack resources for their own purposes, just as other groups can. Whether they have ever done this on a scale comparable to an Enron or a Robert Maxwell is, however, worthy of a moment's consideration. The checks and balances on public sector abuse have always been very substantial. So abuse and professional colonisation of resources has always been constrained and scrutinised.

That having been said, it is my view that one of the salient features of the post-war years of public service provision was a continuing ethos of 'caring professionalism' – a sense of vocation. This sense of mission endured and often ran beyond the practices and special interest already noted above. The very fact that, so often, teaching and nursing was of such a high standard on the back of low pay and inadequate resources speaks volumes about the sense of vocation and duty of many public service workers during these times. I would suggest that we underestimate the self-sacrificing sense of mission of so many public service workers at our peril.

The key point is that public service professions are not monolithic entities. A profession is a 'coalition of interests', held together under a common name at a particular time. Hence, a profession will contain some elements that are self-serving and some that are purely instrumental (even minimalist in their professional ethos), whilst other groups maintain high standards of practice and a dedicated sense of duty and mission. The difficulty, then, is to design reforms and restructuring initiatives that contain, constrain and redirect the self-serving, instrumental and minimalist elements, whilst rewarding and applauding those with a dedicated sense of mission and vocation. This chapter illustrates the fact that reforms have targeted the less public-spirited elements of professionalism but, in doing so, have also demeaned and diminished the sense of mission and public duty that has, for so long, characterised the best of our public service provision. In short, the reforms too often 'throw the baby out with the bathwater' and, once thrown out, the baby will prove uncommonly hard to resuscitate. What is required in reforms around the Western world is some pause in the frenetic pace of restructuring to reflect on the profound dangers that emerge when the dedicated and dutiful groups that underpin our public services begin to voice their alienation and despair in growing numbers.

Only when this happens, and we have some way to go on the learning curve, certainly amongst the Blairite politbureau, can we expect a re-joining of private meaning and public purpose. I await this consummation with trepidation, but enduring hope.

References

Arnold, S. (2001) 'Savage angels', *Observer Review*, 4 February.

Bly, R. (1991) *Iron John*, Shaftesbury: Element Books.

Goodson, I.F. (2003) *Professional Knowledge, Professional Lives, Studies in Education and Change*, Maidenhead: Open University Press.

Goodson, I.F. (2005) *Learning, Curriculum and Life Politics*, London: Routledge.

Goodson, I.F. and Hargreaves, A. (1996) 'Teachers' Professional Lives, Aspirations and Actualities', in I.F. Goodson and A. Hargreaves (eds) *Teachers' Professional Lives*, pp. 1–27, Washington: Falmer Press.

Green, C. (2001) 'The railwayman's lament', *The Guardian*, 14 April.

Harper, K. (2001) 'Excuses, and cash supply, finally ran out', *The Guardian*, 8 October.

Hewitt, B. and Fitzsimons, C. (2001) 'I quit', *Guardian Education*, 9 January.

Ignatieff, M. (2001) 'What will victory be?', *The Guardian*, 4 October.

Leith, W. (2006) 'Diary', *New Statesman*, 9 January.

Levinson, D. (1979) *The Seasons of a Man's Life*, New York: Ballantine Books.

Levinson, D. and Levinson, J. (1996) *The Seasons of a Woman's Life*, New York: Alfred A. Knopf.

Marshall, G. (2001) 'Commentary', *The Observer*, 28 October.

Newnham, D. (1997) 'Going loco', *The Guardian Weekend*, 1 March.

Putnam, R. (2001) *Bowling Alone, the Collapse and Revival of American Community*, New York: Simon & Schuster.

Rifkin, J. (2001) *The Age of Access: How the Shift from Ownership to Access is Transforming Capitalism*, London: Penguin.

Robson, S. (2001) 'Commentary', *The Guardian*, 10 October.

Ross, A. (2001) 'Heads will roll', *Guardian Education*, 23 January.

Sennett, R. (1999) *The Corrosion of Character, the Personal Consequences of Work in the New Capitalism*, London: W.W. Norton.

Sheehy, G. (1998) *Understanding Men's Passages, Discovering the New Map of Men's Lives*, New York: Random House.

Thesiger, W. (2002) 'Wild at heart', *The Guardian*, 29 June.

Troman, G. (1996) 'The rise of the new professionals? The restructuring of primary teachers' work and professionalism', *British Journal of Sociology of Education*, 17(4), 473–87.

9 The educational researcher as public intellectual

The multi-faceted appeal of Lawrence Stenhouse, both to contemporaries and to new generations, is testified to in the wide range of lectures and testimonies that have sought to represent and characterise his work. For me, the central element in his appeal was that in both his writing and his action, he spoke as a public intellectual; as one who expected his ideas to form the basis of influence and action in the public sphere. Moreover, his central concern was with education for empowerment and social justice. In an early draft manifesto for the Centre for Applied Research he stressed its role as a 'public service'. As we shall see, in some senses the times in which he lived brought aid and sustenance to this view of an educational researcher's social and political purpose, but we should also be aware that he also existed in vigorously contested terrains. Towards the end of his life, he must have begun to glimpse the 'dark night' into which much of his vernacular humanism would be cast in the new order, where there was to be 'no such thing as society'.

Public knowledge and public education have historically been subject to recurrent pendulum swings between the emancipatory/Enlightenment vision and the darker forces of subordination and social control. From the point of view of public intellectual life, Thomas Paine expressed the high optimism of the Enlightenment when he argued, 'I am a farmer of thoughts and all the crops I raise I give away.'

Well, we know what the Tory free marketeers would think of that kind of high-mindedness, when only things that are done for profit are pursued or praised. But, in truth, public knowledge and public education have often been subjected to the kind of 'dark night' we have recently been experiencing.

In 1807, the British Parliament debated a bill to provide two years of free schooling for children aged 7–14, who could not pay fees. The Archbishop of Canterbury said it would subvert the first principles of education in his country that had been and, he trusted, would continue to be, under the control of the establishment. One MP, Davies Giddy, is recorded in the 13 July (1807) edition of *Hansard* as having uttered the following prophetic words:

> However specious in theory the project might be of giving education to the labouring classes of the poor, it would be prejudicial to their morals and

happiness; it would teach them to despise their lot in life, instead of making them good servants in agriculture and other laborious employments. Instead of teaching them subordination, it would render them fractious and refractory, as was evident in the manufacturing counties; it would enable them to read seditious pamphlets, vicious books and publications against Christianity; it would render them insolent to their superiors; and in a few years, the legislature would find it necessary to direct the strong arm of power toward them.

(Giddy 1807)

Interestingly, Noam Chomsky has recently invoked the early 1800s as the last time when the rich and powerful and industrial interests had truly unlimited powers. Until now, that is – in his recent Cambridge lecture he said, speaking about the present day:

There has been a recognition on the part of very powerful sectors that they have the population by the throat. They have an opportunity not just to fight a holding action against the increase of human rights and labour rights and democracy, but actually to roll it back and to restore the utopia of the masters of the kind that was dreamed of in the 1820s.

(Chomsky 1995)

David Marquand, in a slightly more diplomatic manner, has described the characteristics of a typical Conservative government minister:

The most obvious hallmark of the Thatcher and Major governments has been a ferocious onslaught on institutional autonomy, diversity and stability in the name of the rationality of the marketplace. Almost all the institutions which used to shield an unusually stable and diverse civil society from the arrogance of the politicians in temporary command of the state, or which embodied values and practices at variance with those of market economies, have felt the lash of this Tory Jacobinism ... One result is that the core executive at the heart of this state – the tiny group of senior ministers and top officials who make up the elective dictatorship which governs Britain – has to reckon with fewer countervailing powers than ever before in peacetime.

(Marquand 1994)

Now, the notion that the pendulum swings with regard to public knowledge is itself an ideological position, for there are certainly those, at the moment, who argue for the 'end of history' and, indeed, Chomsky himself has come close to this view. Whilst the 'end of history' is plainly an absurd notion when taken literally, it does question whether the current reallocation of global power constitutes a phase of culmination in the long march of the rich and powerful. If this were so, the assumption that the pendulum will one day swing back to more emancipated notions of education has at least to be questioned, if not as yet finally dismissed. If the 'end of history' fails to capture the nuances, then certainly the end of hope – of particular hopes such as social justice or redistribution – comes close to the mark. For the moment, as you will see, my position echoes the character in *Boys from the Blackstuff* who, at the end of his life, still said 'I just can't believe there's no hope'.

The reason for starting with this rather broad canvas of commentary is that issues affecting educational research (whether as public intellectual work or not) are clearly affected by the current changes in the global economy. As education and schooling are themselves repositioned and re-stratified in the new global work order, so inevitably, research on education is itself repositioned. In such a situation, even if people go on researching as they researched before, their work may have been repositioned; sometimes so as to substantially shift or even invert the relevance and effect of that work. The recent changes in the global economy thus work at a number of levels – at levels of economic production, there is a much-analysed 'crisis of modernisation' and a consequent need to explore and interrogate the condition of post-modernity, but at levels of cultural production, it is to the above 'crisis of positionality' that we should be turning. A crisis of positionality arises at this point because high modern capital has successfully reconstituted and repositioned the social relations of production: the newly deregulated circulation of capital globally, substantially confines and repositions those social movements that have sought to tackle issues of redistribution and inequality. Welfare states, national trade unions, progressive movements and so on can be redefined by a press of the button, which moves capital from 'intransigent' national and local sites (economically inefficient sites) to more malleable sites (economically competitive sites). Global capital thus has a twin triumph to celebrate: the emasculation of social democratic/egalitarian movements within the Western world and the culminating destruction of alternative systems of production and distribution in the Communist world. These twin triumphs leave would-be public intellectuals in a precarious and rudderless position – detached from past histories of action for social justice and divorced from hard-won visions of alternative futures. In the crisis of positionality, there is no firm ground to stand on and to remain in the same place is to risk one's position being changed nonetheless.

Locating the public intellectual

In locating Lawrence Stenhouse's role as a public intellectual and in scrutinising the changing terrain of the last 30 or so years, it is, I think, particularly instructive to examine the trajectory of the Centre for Applied Research in Education. The Centre was founded by Stenhouse in 1970, but grew out of the Humanities Curriculum Project (HCP), which began in 1967.

HCP drew deeply on the egalitarian commitments of sections of post-war British society. The 'we're all in it together' spirit of the war emanated from attempts to build a New Jerusalem under the Labour governments of 1945–51. Whilst watered down by subsequent governments, these social justice sentiments were still alive and well in the mid-1960s, when the HCP was conceived. The spirit is well captured in one of the first Schools Council working papers on raising the school leaving age:

> The problem is to give every man some access to a complex cultural inherit ance, some hold on his personal life and on his relationships with the various communities to which he belongs, some extension of his understanding of, and sensitivity towards, other human beings. The aim is to forward understanding, discrimination and judgement in the human field – it will involve reliable factual knowledge, where this is appropriate, direct experience, imaginative experience, some appreciation of the dilemmas of the human condition, of the rough-hewn nature of many of our institutions and some rational thought about them.
>
> (Schools Council 1965)

That such sentiments could be expressed by establishment figures in 1960s Britain shows that some powerful groups in society were committed to continuing egalitarian projects. It should be remembered that, at almost the same time in the USA, Lyndon Johnson was launching his 'Great Society' initiative. So, far from building an egalitarian fortress, Britain was, in fact, part of a broader world movement. Noel Annan has written in his book, *Our Age*, of the substantial support within the liberal elements of the British establishment for social justice (Annan 1995). He judges that *Our Age* lasted from 1945 until well into the 1970s.

One of the offshoots of the social justice movement was the curriculum development movement in schools – seeking to broaden educational opportunities for *all* pupils. As MacDonald recalls:

> In England, it was largely the lower reaches of the education system that constituted the recruiting grounds of innovation – the colleges of teacher training and the schools themselves. For these upwardly mobile but academically under-qualified recruits, there was no ready-made entry into the discipline-based heights of the institutional order. The universities had not been party to the political settlement that saw the ministry, the local authorities and the teacher unions sink their differences over curriculum control in the tri-partite Schools Council.
>
> Thus it was that the patrons and minders of the early innovators, or at least of the more eminent members thereof, saw the need to secure a future for them. Wheels turned and deals were struck. One of them led to the setting up of the Centre for Applied Research in Education (CARE) at the University of East Anglia, which (and this was thought to be a blessing at the time) had no school of education. This kind of package deal (tenured university posts for four people who didn't have two PhDs to rub together) implanted in higher education the 'seeds of its reconstruction' – in my view, the totally unintended but most significant and lasting impact of the curriculum development movement.
>
> (MacDonald 1991)

CARE thus provided a think-tank for curriculum development and school innovation and evaluation projects. The work was powered by the political settlements of the day and by the support of substantial elements in the liberal establishment, as well as the broader Labour movement and other movements committed to social justice. At this time, then, educational researchers at CARE could act as public intellectuals since, in a sense, they were working with the grain of support from these social movements. It is always difficult to stand at one historical moment and recreate a sense of the past, but MacDonald has captured the heady sense of momentum in the early days of CARE:

> The curriculum development projects of the 1960s (by the end of the decade some 200 national initiatives had been funded) led, in the 1970s, to a re-staffing of a still expanding system (the school leaving age was raised to 16 in 1972) on a new basis – the experience of change.
>
> [...] They poured into the departments of education in the universities and the polytechnics, the local authority advisory services, even the national inspectorate and senior school positions, bringing to their new responsibilities a hands-on knowledge of the practice of schooling that would breathe new life into those atrophied institutions by challenging their traditions and offering them a new role. The beachheads of an unfamiliar academic territory were rapidly established in higher education, increasingly under the title of 'curriculum studies'. The theoretical tradition of education based on derivative disciplines began to give way to the new theorists of educational practice whose theory was based on the close observation of new curricula in action, grounded theory of school life whose conceptual catholicity and seemingly casual disregard for the carefully constructed authority of the social sciences had to meet and survive accusations of amateurism and naive ignorance. But survive and flourish they did, not least because, supported by their colleagues in the local authority advisory services, they exerted an increasingly decisive role in the reshaping of in-service education for teachers, taking that opportunity to draw their students into the process of field-based enquiry into school problems and practices. That opportunity was extended as more and more colleges of initial training were incorporated into the institutions of higher education.
>
> (MacDonald 1991)

In such a climate as this, the power of ideas is considerable. These initiatives represent a sense of 'a world under construction'. The public sector of schooling was being reconstructed and educational research provided important insights into this process. When public services are being re-conceptualised and reconstructed in helpful and broadly supportive ways by sympathetic politicians, the educational researcher as public intellectual emerges from the shadows.

But this social democratic moment was about to be extinguished. In their powerful book, *'Goodbye, Great Britain'*, Kathleen Burk and Alec Cairncross give an insider's view of the financial and economic events of 1976 (Burk and Cairncross 1992). Broadly speaking, the International Monetary Fund pronounced an end to the social projects of post-war Britain. But this was again part of a broader world movement that saw Western economies in the wake of the oil crisis of 1973 begin to struggle with new realities as the long post-war boom came to an end.

As we have seen, movements for social justice had developed sectors of support within the British establishment, but such a programme was never likely to win the hearts and minds of the rich and powerful, of those representing industrial and multinational interests. The advocates of the 'free market' emerged from the spawning think-tanks of the 1970s to define a programme that revised the projects of post-war Britain. The role of the public intellectual shifted towards these groups and, in doing so, left centres like CARE detached from the axes of power and policy. This crisis of positionality was to grow as the New Right programme gathered momentum and new adherents. CARE continued to function and to undertake major projects, but what was progressively lost was the link to an overarching social project that expressed the humanistic vision of the founding members. More and more research projects were generated in response to 'offers to tender' rather than conceived of for their public and moral purposes. New projects on police training, new technology and nurse training were undertaken. The rationales for such project work were forced to become more and more pragmatic and thereby less and less infused with broader visions of social justice.

The 1980s and early 1990s has been described in various ways within CARE. One member argued that the project was 'to follow the fireball of New Right policies wherever they go [...] documenting and analysing the effects' (Saville Kushner, personal communication January 1966).

Another senior member at CARE noted, with more humility, that the Centre was going through a period of 'hibernation' but would, in due course, emerge from its burrow into the light of day.

In fact, in the 1980s, as has been noted, major proposals in the fields of police training, the health services, the media, libraries and schools were undertaken. The commitment to researching and evaluating public services continued. As one member said, 'I've not given up on modernism yet!' (B. Macdonald, personal communication, 8 February 1986).

Indeed, when I joined CARE in 1994 on sabbatical and subsequently on a permanent basis, I was struck by the continuing force of the value system with regard to social justice and social projects. It was as if a collective memory of a more decent and compassionate Britain, what was described as 'a Britain that cares', continued to inform the work. But if the collective memory continued to provide moral guidance, what was palpable was the absence of social movements, or indeed social moments, in which to locate this value position.

A hibernating collective memory grafted to a pragmatic programme of research and evaluation in a hostile world might summarise CARE in the 1990s. Like Sartre throughout his life, CARE appeared to be waiting.

The dominant motif of CARE in the 1990s was a series of pragmatic projects still committed to, and concerned with, a basic vernacular humanism. What was missing was the overarching social movement that had been provided through the post-war egalitarian project. At one level, one might say, in post-modern fashion, that all that was lost was a myth, a rhetoric of progress, a linear and unifying progress narrative, a masculine, middle class, mid-life, meritocratic, mythological muddle passing itself off as a high moral purpose.

But as I hope I've showed, the egalitarian project moved beyond discourses to mobilise and motivate substantial and influential sections of British society. We should therefore beware of limiting our understanding to discourse analysis and deconstruction, for it would be to misread and misrepresent a major period of reconstruction and struggle in British public life. The collective memory of that struggle still provides 'resources for hope' as we face the need to build new pro-grammes and projects for millennial Britain. Specifically in CARE, the collec-tive memory of humanistic egalitarianism remains strong and will infuse the search to reconstitute projects of social justice.

Relocating public education

So, to summarise the previous section, the 'we're all in it together' socialism of the post-war governments settled into a balanced, partially egalitarian project until the mid-1970s. This temporary political settlement (which covered both parties for a time) allowed educational researchers to conduct policy-linked pub-lic intellectual work. It was the collapse of the egalitarian project that severed the link between public intellectual work and an overarching project of social justice. Although the collapse has taken place over the last 20 years, I believe we are only now beginning to face the implications and undertaking the task of rebuilding alliances and perspectives.

The implications for what E.P. Thompson called the *égalité* of this collapse of a social movement have been painfully rendered in an article that he wrote whilst in an NHS ward, recovering from the disease that was to kill him:

> What makes me feel old, also, is the realisation that what I had thought to be widely held principles are now little more than quaint survivals among the least flexible of my generation. We had supposed, quite fiercely, that one didn't try to bend the rules. If people wanted to pay for convenience or for extras – good spectacles or special dentures or nursing home deliveries or convalescent comfort – we could go along with that. But access to the essen-tial resources of the service must be ruled by *égalité*. And we believed that professional people (those who were socialists) should be loyal to this most of all. For if they started buying private latchkeys, then the whole system would start to get fouled up with the double standards and hierarchies of class. Times and manners have changed. The generation which fought for the NHS, and which has now come to that stage of life where they need it most, must jostle with the assertive anti-moralistic young. Everyone is into latchkeys, technicians and skilled workers as well. If my wife and I and a few friends want to hold out for old 'principles' no one is going to stop us. But I have to recognise now that such a stiff-backed sense of honour could cost

even risk to one's life. And if we still choose to be like that, can one possibly make the same choice for another – a child or a grandchild? And by what right?

One is left with a 'principle' that the young can't even understand, which is ineffectual (unless self-damaging), and which is really a private notion of honour. Or a stuffy habit of the old. And I suddenly can see the survivors of that socialist age-cohort as historical relics, like the old Covenantor in *The Heart of Midlothian*. Those of us who stay loyal to the old imperatives and taboos – the oaths of *égalité* – are a goldmine for the oral historian, and Raphael Samuel will collect us as specimens in a nostalgic book.

(Thompson 1987)

The ritual death of the *égalité* at the hands of the market poses the classic 'problem of positionality' for humanistic caring professionals trying to 'stand in the same place'. The health professionals who had inhabited a humane micro-world, dispensing health services to *all* according to need, found that their work was repositioned into dispensing something else altogether. So a nurse could be working on the same ward in the same hospital throughout the two decades of Tory reconstruction, but by the end, the positional significance of that work had been transformed. One could tell similar stories of probation officers, social workers, comprehensive schoolteachers and indeed educational researchers.

But let me return to Lawrence Stenhouse and to CARE, because it is here that we can interrogate some of the problems of positionality.

During the 1970s, besides conducting a wide range of curriculum development and evaluation projects, CARE became a centre for defining educational research modalities in the public sphere. I have argued that egalitarian social movements offered aid and sustenance to educational research pursuing goals of social justice. But now the downside of this social movement has to be confronted. For it is here we view the essential crisis of positionality. What might in another sense be called the 'paradox of progressivism'.

Being interlinked and embedded in a wider political project for social justice, for an education of inclusion, a schooling that would seek to empower and enlighten all sections of society produced its own points of blindness. For as MacDonald notes: 'We the innovators began under benign and supportive government and saw the problem largely as a technical one, under professional control' (MacDonald 1991).

The task for CARE, then, was to find intellectual answers to the problem of empowering education for all. This assumption of benign governance came from the salience of the egalitarian project in some establishment circles. CARE proceeded on a belief in good intentions, a secure sense of good faith and a belief in the moral high ground of work to educate all sections of society. This belief was to have profound consequences, for it led into definitions of educational research that could be hijacked, perverted and repositioned for other social and political purposes. Because of the belief in governmental good intentions and in the ideological supremacy of egalitarianism, patterns of educational research remained depoliticised and detached from concepts of power. Again, MacDonald has cogently reflected on the 30-year moratorium that followed 1945:

> The development of a political consciousness in education was delayed by 30 years. The post-war expansion of schooling was powered by a political consensus around the notion of Keynesian social democracy. Throughout that period, it seemed that economic buoyancy would finance the agreed goals of full employment, adequate social services, and the co-existence of public and private enterprise. In 1970, expenditure on education exceeded expenditure on defence for the first, but last time. The writing was now on the wall (and the Schools Council under severe political attack as the warning signs were taken heed of) and recession looming. The consensus collapsed under Labour in the mid to late 1970s in a massive failure of adaption to the new economic realities. The truce was over, as was the indulgence. The politics of moderation were out, the politics of extremism in. The sense of a failing society (with schooling, of course, a favourite target) was pervasive, and of a failing socialism, conclusive. In an extraordinary ideological coup (not least of her own party), Thatcher seized the opportunity to introduce and implement a version of economic liberalism not seen since the nineteenth century – the undistorted market.
>
> (MacDonald 1991: 12)

This sense of good intentions led to a form of 'progressive overreach', whereby strong liberal and entrenched positions were overthrown in the search for more egalitarian and more inclusive modalities. In the progressive moment, confident of benign government, with an expansionist economy and social democratic movements seeking to counter the allure of communism, this 'reaching for more' was profoundly understandable. Hence, 'applied research' was a central mantra of CARE in the early 1970s. Applied research sought to move beyond the liberal discourse of foundational theory in teacher education. Writing in 1974 in a paper on the future of CARE, Lawrence noted:

> About 15 years ago an attack was mounted on the intellectual standard of the teaching of education in universities and colleges. This attack stressed the need to teach education through its 'constituent disciplines'. Philosophy, psychology and sociology won a central place. History and comparative education were more peripheral. This attack carried the day and majority of courses in education in both universities and colleges are now founded in the constituent disciplines.
>
> (Stenhouse, CARE Discussion paper 1974)

The group working in CARE are united in a reaction against this, the predominant tradition at present. Whilst not questioning the intellectual standard of the work being done in the constituent disciplines, we question its practical relevance. Holding that we understand too little of the educational process at policy, school and classroom levels, we are evolving methodologies for the study of the realities of educational systems. The emphasis is not unique to CARE, but I would claim that the CARE group is the most advanced unit of its kind in this country and that it has now developed a tradition that is characteristic

(CARE 1974)

For the moment, I want to stay with Lawrence's diagnosis before returning to applied research as the solution. I've been spending a good deal of time recently thinking about the role of educational theory in schools. The focus on disciplined educational theory arose from the location of many schools of education within the university milieu. Clifford and Guthrie have summarised the differences that Lawrence was focusing on in the 1970s in this way:

Our thesis is that schools of education, particularly those located on the campuses of prestigious research universities, have become ensnared improvidently in the academic and political cultures of their institutions and have neglected their professional allegiances. They are like marginal men, aliens in their own worlds. They have seldom succeeded in satisfying the scholarly norms of their campus letters and science colleagues, and they are simultaneously estranged from their practising professional peers. The more forcefully they have rowed toward the shores of scholarly research, the more distant they have become from the public schools they are duty bound to serve. Conversely, systematic efforts at addressing the applied problems of public schools have placed schools of education at risk on their own campuses.

(Clifford and Guthrie 1988)

In short, schools may have entered into a 'devil's bargain' when they entered the university milieu. The result was that their mission changed from being primarily concerned with matters central to the practice of schooling, towards issues of status passage through more conventional university scholarship. The resulting dominance of conventional 'disciplinary' modes has had a disastrous impact on educational research.

It may not be true that, as Adam Smith said, 'every profession is a conspiracy against the people'; it is, however, certainly true that professional groups construct their 'missions' in terms of the pursuit of status and resources as well as ideals. Hence, faculties of education have codified and created bodies of knowledge to maximise the terms of the 'devil's bargain'. Bodies of knowledge were created with two major functions: first, the creation of a corpus of 'expert knowledge', with which to instruct trainee teachers; second, and closely allied to this, bodies of knowledge were designed to maximise status and esteem within the university milieu. Disciplinary theory served both purposes and symbolically enshrined the essentially academic and scholarly purposes of the faculties of education. If a side-effect of these strategies was to reduce field-based inquiry and collaboration, this, it seems, was once judged a price worth paying.

Hence the question of whether educational research is worthwhile is one of great importance. C. Wright Mills, I think, comes close to the nature of our dilemma and spells out the implications of the devil's bargain when he talks about the way that 'men of knowledge' orient themselves to 'special segments of society'. This has been the fate of much educational and curriculum theory and the effect has been that, as Mills puts it, different groups 'talk past each other' (Mills 1979). With few exceptions, I would argue this is precisely the relationship between faculties of education and school practitioners: they constitute a model of how to talk past each other.

The crucial point to grasp, however, is that the communication and ongoing displacement between theory and practice is not an intrinsic, but rather a socially structured, problem. New structures of collaboration and forms of knowledge might rapidly ease the current problems.

It was to solve some of these problems that Lawrence Stenhouse developed a notion of applied research. But I think the reaction to disciplinary theory went too far and, as we shall see, although no one could have foreseen this, the timing was bad. The issue was not to dismantle theory altogether but to replace foundational theory with a more engaged theory/practice equation.

However, applied research aimed to evacuate foundational theory in order to immerse itself in the realities of classroom life. In the process, though, the capacity of foundational and disciplinary theory to address broad questions about the historical, sociological and philosophical definition of schooling was potentially lost. Under benign governance and believing in good intentions – classrooms and compassionate and would-be democratic micro-worlds – these were the places to be located, and in which to conduct and generate applied research. What was lost in a welter of good intentions was the public intellectual handle on questions of the social position, the ideological content, the grammar, the social epistemology, the social and political place and purpose of schooling. Applied research in classrooms is fine when classrooms are progressing, becoming more inclusive, more democratic places. But when the tide turned, applied research suffered from extreme *discourse deficit*. The focus on application on classrooms left educational research a victim of those who could redefine applications and classrooms. Applied research was left with too few levers to look at the overarching questions that were once explored, albeit patchily, in foundational theory.

Moreover, the applied research movement, by aiding in the dissolution and deconstruction of foundational theory, helped soften up the context for a wholly different ideological coup of the sort MacDonald refers to. By focusing back on practice, especially to classroom practices, the doors were open to a new, more utilitarian, doctrine of teacher education and educational research. Teaching and schooling could now be presented as practical matters that were beyond broad intellectual contestation. And if teaching is a practical matter, then changing schooling is a matter of technical fine-tuning and education research is only there to service the technical adjustments that will deliver effective schools.

The paradox of progressivism in the era of 1970s CARE is that by helping dismantle the liberal settlement of foundational and disciplinary theory to move towards a more engaged and practical applied research mode, a wholly different ideological coup was facilitated. By 1980, the forces that had long contested empowering education for all were in control and their desire to extinguish educational theory, which engaged questions of the nature and purposes of schooling, was evident. For them, all arguments for applied and practical research helped to obscure the larger question of social purpose and social allocation. Progressive arguments were hijacked, inverted and used for a wholly indifferent social project, with diametrically opposed purposes.

Now in case this sounds too glib – which it does – and too critical of applied research, I should note that it is symptomatic of the broad-based paradox of progressivism in this period – of a crisis of positionality not of one's own making and which could not have been fully foreseen. Certainly I don't want to risk self-abuse in this chapter, but I should note that much of my own work on school knowledge falls fairly and squarely into the positional trap I have defined, as do most other progressive modalities and practices conceived of in the 30 years since 1945. To say this is to confirm the extent of the task of re-conceptualisation and repositioning that stands before us. But there is a final paradox – whilst flawed and ultimately enmeshed in the positional trap defined above, the work of groups like CARE still provides the kind of collective memory and sets of working definitions and practices that will be invaluable in rebuilding new projects, which aim at social justice and social enlightenment. As always in social change, we have to pick ourselves up and begin again. This time a little wiser, less believing in governmental and global good intentions, and more cognisant of the need for 'theories of evil', as we pursue our purposes.

So far you may have discovered some level of modernist longing in this argument – so there is a whiff of the modernist dinosaur – but there is also a sense of the dangerous delusions of modernism, which lead into so many positional traps. Those dangerous delusions were sponsored in a period of expansionist economic reconstruction, where more socially inclusive policies were temporarily promised.

In this period, notions of the public sphere and of intellectual work – and specifically education research, which applied itself to improving public life – were readily accessible. But in the last 20 years, there has been a profound struggle for public life and for the intellectual work associated with its improvement.

Lest we accept that it is a problem of shortage of money, it is worth pointing out that the opposite is happening to the police, the army and to expenditure on military weapons and private developments, like shopping malls and housing. Here there is a huge growth in expenditure and in expanding developments.

Overall, then, we are obviously not short of money. What is happening is that we are consistently choosing the private over the public at nearly all levels and this is playing through into an attack on the median level.

Wolf argues that the median levels of professional life are a confusing nuisance between the direct relationship of the state and its subjects and industry and its customers. In the median level critique, social criticism, theory building and arguments against inequality still reside.

Therefore, the attempt, at the global level, is to weaken this level and move the centre of action for knowledge construction to other levels. Michael Gibbons has recently written about the distinction between mode 1 and mode 2 knowledge. Mode 1 knowledge is essentially disciplinary knowledge – normally developed in the traditional universities. Mode 2 knowledge is applied knowledge, and is increasingly developed in the R&D sectors of the private industrial base, together with the think-tanks associated with this sector of the economy. Whilst mode 1 knowledge is under sustained attack, mode 2 knowledge is being sponsored. This is merely a version of the changing priority from public to private that I mentioned earlier.

I am trying to deal with these other questions in work that I am undertaking at the moment. One way to sidestep the whole question is to embrace the definition of intellectuals provided in the *Dictionary of Scientific Quotations*. Tadeusz Kotarbinski is credited with the quote: 'an intellectual is a parasite that exudes culture' (Kotarbinski 1997).

So if the public aspect of the public intellectual seems increasingly perilous under post-modernity, let us examine the place of intellectuals more generally. In Britain this place has, of course, always been contested, whether within modernity or after modernity.

However, Noel Annan (1995) judges that post-war academics enjoyed a golden age of influence – he argues that the period up until 1975 was the 'Age of the Don'. Certainly, as we have seen in the case of CARE, there was, for a period, a fruitful exchange between parts of the political establishment and educational researchers – public policy and public intellectual work were briefly linked. But when the establishment changes side, as happened in the 1970s, the role of the public intellectual becomes instantly questionable in terms of the humanistic values expressed by those such as Stenhouse. A.H. Halsey has also ruminated on this matter in a recent book about the academic world. He judges that British academics fall into two groups. The largest is a group whose members consider themselves to be employed in increasingly specialist professions, with a primarily conservative emphasis.

First, this somewhat heterogeneous collection of increasingly specialist professions is, in a cultural sense, conservative. This conservatism reflects in part the distinctive character of secure attachment to the state and the social order, which has earned the description of the British 'key' profession as pragmatic and useful – a ready servant of government administration and industrial need.

No one wishes to be labelled an intellectual, and worse, the intelligentsia is often perceived as a dated, obscure class of possibly foreign dissidents. Anti-intellectualism in this sense has been a feature of British culture at least since the reform and revival of the universities by the Victorians. The structure of British society has offered continually renewed support for these sentiments. There are professional rewards for specialists both within the academic world and outside in the House of Lords, the boardrooms of industrial companies, the mass media, the governing bodies of quangos and even the political parties. There have been, in short, powerfully integrating forces working to make scientists and scholars 'at home' in their society (Halsey 1992).

Halsey notes that what he calls the high professors, 'The leading one tenth of academic staff', are disproportionately the highest qualified in terms of first-class degrees and disproportionately more productive (ibid.: 252). They are also disproportionately linked to the establishment – a fifth of all high professors are privately schooled, as opposed to 7 per cent of the general population. Halsey wrote:

> Oxford and Cambridge, with their close ties both in recruitment from the well-to-do and as suppliers to the elevated metropolitan institutions of State and Industry, are also dominantly the nurseries of both the intellectuals and the powers. Such a pattern of connection has undoubtedly given Britain an integrated establishment of political, economic, and cultural management.
>
> (Ibid.)

Moreover, he notes that the high professors are to the right of their colleagues, 'both in their subjective place on the political spectrum and their voting record' (ibid.: 256).

However, Halsey also notes that, as always in British life, there exists across the academic world what Orwell called 'the awkward squad' – a group that refuses hegemony for one reason or another, ranging from leftish commitment through to personal refusal.

Of course, it would be wrong to equate intellectuals with academics. But, since the word 'intellectual' first emerged in Russia to characterise nihilistic university students, more and more intellectual life has been colonised by the massive expansion of universities. Edward Shils describes intellectuals as 'persons with unusual sensitivity to the sacred, an uncommon reflectiveness about the nature of their universe and the rules which govern society' (Shils 1972).

In the past, they have found patrons as disparate as royalty, the aristocracy, the church, the army, newspapers, the media, the welfare state and beggars. But, as Halsey notes, nowadays we are forced to the conclusion that 'institutions of higher education are their major institutional location' (Halsey 1992: 252).

Raymond Williams spent much of his life railing against the conservative bias of the academic world, which he judged to be a central explanation of what he called 'English backwardness':

> He makes the acid point that those who could be called intellectuals in other countries are in Britain mostly brought up in a system of private education designed for a class which includes the leading politicians, civil servants, company directors and lawyers.
>
> (Williams 1983)

Williams' diagnosis of late 1980s Britain is a depressing one:

> At every level, including our own, this is a seriously undereducated society. The problems it faces are intractable with the kind of information and

argument now publicly available. There is no obvious way of measuring this most serious of deficits. Some indications occur in the condition of our newspapers after a hundred years of general literacy, and in the character of parliamentary and electoral debates. The way is open for weak minds to renounce, in some despair, the whole project of public education.

(Williams 1989: 21)

Revisiting public education

Following Williams, let me then revisit the question of educational research, the public intellectual and, indeed, the issues of public education. For we face a contradiction: Halsey and Williams find an English intelligentsia that is either complicit with power or marginalised, but Annan reminds us that, up until 1975, there was, in some sense, a golden age of influence. As we have seen in the earlier examination of CARE, this confluence was often on the side not of power, but of social justice.

Clearly, the 'we're all in it together' socialism of the post-war governments settled into a balanced egalitarian project until the mid-1970s. This temporary political settlement (which covered both parties for a time) allowed educational researchers to conduct policy-linked public intellectual work. It was the collapse of the egalitarian project that severed the link between public intellectual work and an overarching project of social justice.

In some ways, the changes to a market-based system challenge the very assumptions of post-war public life as, of course, they were intended to do. Public services wither, the public sector contracts and in a broader sense public life is diminished. This attack on things 'public' transforms the prospects for public life and public action. The attack on public space is intimately linked with the prospects of public intellectual engagement. Geoff Mulgan and Ken Worpole have spent a good deal of time surveying these changes and conclude that:

> A profound change has overcome our public spaces. Only half the population now dares to go out after dark, fewer than a third of children are allowed to walk to school, and public fear of strangers regularly erupts after such public murders as Jamie Bulger and Rachel Nickell. Clearly this is not a nation at ease with itself.
>
> But while the parks, railway stations and many side streets are full of boarded-up stalls, toilets and kiosks, billions of pounds have been pumped into glossy shopping centres such as Newcastle's Metro Centre and Sheffield's Meadowhall. Their virtue is that they offer security through control: no eating allowed except in designated spaces, no litter permitted, there is no weather, no running about and no dogs.
>
> (Mulgan and Worpole 1994: 24)

They might have added, as a recent US legal test confirmed, that since shopping malls are private spaces, no public political activities can be undertaken within them – hence a woman organising a petition for a local community project was judged to be acting illegally. One begins to wonder what would be the status of an intellectual-cum-political conversation in a shopping mall – would this also be illegal? In the event, the owners have normally precluded such prospects – the muzak normally drives out the prospect of such talk, let alone thought. Suzanne Moore summarises the effect of the changing public/private balance on political and moral thought:

> the valorisation of private property that took place in the eighties produced an almost tangible disdain for anything that was not privately owned. As a psychic state, this was tolerable, but when people saw it enacted in their cities, schools and hospitals, the decay of public space, bad enough in itself, became symbolic of something even more rotten at the heart of the government. To talk of civic society, never mind civic duty, is difficult among broken-down playgrounds littered with old condoms and screwed-up tin foil, lifts that don't work, streets you wouldn't want your children to roam.
>
> (Moore 1994: 5)

In France, the dilemma can be more easily understood. In the Latin Quarter of Paris, intellectuals gathered in the post-war period around a cluster of bookshops, cafes and bars. In her memoires, Simone de Beauvoir captured this time when:

> Journalists, authors and would-be film-makers discussed, projected and decided with passion, as though their future depended upon them.
>
> But now the bookshops have been replaced with chic fashion stores. The cafes have likewise become chic, with industrialists and actors as the main clientele. Now the house prices are among the highest in Paris. The people who come here no longer belong to the academic world. They are people who earn a lot of money.
>
> (De Beauvoir 1963)

Marcel Gauchet, a philosopher and editor of the review *Le Debat*, says:

> The cafes are only the most visible aspect of this. The Sorbonne has completely changed and the students who go there are now entirely depoliticised: more than half the bookshops have shut, and the publishing houses are also leaving. For years this was the area that carried intellectual trends. Now, there might still be the odd author, the odd star, but there are no trends.
>
> [...] The changes to the Latin Quarter reflect changes to the position of intellectuals in France and their obliteration from the political scene.
>
> (Gauchet 1994: 20)

Part of the problem of positionality and of developing a strategy for renewal is how to reconnect with the project that began with the 'we're all in it together' spirit of the 1940s and continued in the egalitarian projects of the 1970s.

Since 1979, this sense of collective social purpose has been under systematic attack.

In a crowded island, such a change in the ethos of the establishment has important implications for intellectuals located in the academic world, for the quickest route to funds and fame has always been sucking up to the establishment, even becoming part of the educational establishment. Hedgers and trimmers always proliferate in such closely patrolled circumstances as exist in a small crowded island. Since 1979 they have not just proliferated; they have been richly rewarded. As soon as the deeply flawed National Curriculum was pronounced, there were those who rushed forward with guides and advice on how to implement this monument to iniquity. This form of collaboration has been richly rewarded.

But there was another feature of the crowded island that, I think, will return us inevitably to the compassionate 'there is such a thing as society' view, which underpins egalitarianism. It is quite simply very difficult to escape 'those dreadful people', as one Tory minister called members of the public who travel on British Rail. In a crowded island, beggars can be damned, as they were by Jack Straw, but they can't be banished. In *Revolt of the Elites*, Lasch (1995) has shown how, in America, the elite, intellectuals included, have sought to escape all public commitments and public space. That option is not available on a crowded island – you can seek to demolish national rail services and national bus services, but the resulting traffic jams catch the rich as well as the poor. So in the end, public transport will have to be reinvented and reinvigorated. It will prove to be the same with much of public life – which has been under assault for 18 years. And with the revival of public life and public services, with the revival of that which is public, may come the revival of opportunities for would-be public intellectuals.

Reinventing public intellectual work as education

Broadly speaking, I have divided the experience of would-be public intellectuals into two forms. In the 1960s and 1970s, those working for social justice undertook intellectual work against the background of a 'world under construction' – thought and action remained allied and the link to policy remained close enough for intellectuals to move beyond mere word games.

In the 1980s and early 1990s, those intellectuals working for social justice in education faced a 'world under deconstruction' – many of the most dearly held projects were dismantled or came under sustained attack. In this later period, detached from action and divorced from policy, the public intellectual was forced into an increasingly detached position of arguing through words for policies and activities that were subject to what Ball has rightly observed as a 'discourse of decision'. This is a harsh terrain to occupy, yet there are many examples of people who continued to argue for social justice in race, gender and class terms.

I am reminded of a film I recently watched on the American Civil War. As the South was progressively defeated, less and less land was occupied – just a few towns and strips of land. In the end, the commentator said that all that was left was a 'confederacy of the mind' – a collective memory of an aspiration.

In some ways, that has been the fate of movements for social justice and of associated intellectual work in the past two decades. But we should not underestimate the 'confederacy of the mind'. For one assertion I will make with great force is that the largest problem the attempted reconstruction of the past two decades – the attempt to demolish the Welfare State – has faced is people's 'collective memory' of good public services, of commitments to provision for all, whether it be schools or hospitals. The vital task now is to reinvigorate, reenergise and reinvent new projects and programmes for social justice; for memories and predispositions in Britain remain remarkably resilient. We should now be looking to define a new role for the educational researcher in millennial Britain and we should do so in ways informed by collective memories of social justice initiatives. This should hopefully presage a new investigation of the role of the educational researcher as public intellectual, moving us into a new phase after the optimistic years of the 1960s and early 1970s and the reversal in the two decades that followed. Now we can hope again that there are post-modern prospects to explore. I should note that I'm not talking about re-establishing some old master narrative of social justice – more a set of voices and visions, a moving mosaic of intentions and plans.

Win Breines' distinction between pre-figurative and strategic politics is relevant here. 'Pre-figurative politics seeks to create and sustain within the lived practice of the movement relationships and political forms that "prefigure" and embody the desired society' (Breines 1980: 421). National Health Service hospitals or in pioneering comprehensive schools might be such pre-figurative sites for work. Here, involvement in policy and practice and the pursuit of ideals of social justice might all be pursued in tandem.

In the past 20 years many of these pre-figurative sites have been subject to severe disruption, if not dissolution. In these circumstances pre-figurative practice and policy are, to say the least, difficult. A kind of 'piecemeal pragmatism' becomes the norm but without any energising or inspiring overall visions. We are left working on bits of the mosaic, but with no sense of what it might finally look like or even if we will like the overall plan that emerges. Under 'piecemeal pragmatism' our public intellectual work often falls into the category of 'micro-political contestation' when we get involved in seeking to defend pre-figurative practices or support those who are working to engender or maintain these practices and policies. Alternatively, we involve ourselves in more traditional adversarial academic work developing 'critiques' of the rationales and roots of contemporary public work, driven by imperatives of the market.

This draws us back to Breines' second category of work – strategic politics. 'Strategic politics is concerned with building organisations in order to achieve power so that structural change in the political economic and social order might be achieved' (ibid.: 422). This work is now pressing if new conceptions of service and education for social justice are to emerge – if new pre-figurative activities and sites are to be created. For this to happen, our work must develop from past collective memory to defuse new visions and structures of education for achieving social justice. There are a number of places that we might begin.

In terms of strategic politics, why might there be a chance of a new period for educational research? What are the grounds for hope? Well, just as I have argued that there was progressive overreach in the early 1970s, so I think there has been substantial 'New Right overreach' in the past two decades.

Let me concentrate on three examples of overreach. First, there has been a sustained attack on the professions and on public life generally. In some ways in this period there has been a consistent attempt to alter the public/private balance in one society. The flux in the balance between public and private, between the state and civil society, makes it a particularly difficult time to arbitrate over the place of public intellectual work in educational research and elsewhere. In some ways, the changing balance echoes the American experience summarised by J.K. Galbraith as a move towards 'private wealth and public squalor'. Public life and institutions come under withering attack.

The arguments of Alan Wolf carry considerable weight with me. Wolf has argued that what we are seeing globally is an attack on what he calls the 'median level'. By the median level, he means the public institutions: schools, universities, public broadcasting, libraries, hospitals and so on. In most countries, these institutions are coming under attack and this is evidenced by the fact that less and less is being spent on them.

John Gray has argued that a similar attack on median institutions, as denoted by Wolf, is at work in Britain:

> the Tory nationalisation of Britain's intermediary institutions (the universities, the NHS, even the prosecution service) has demolished the complex structure of checks and balances on which in the past we relied upon for public protection against the abuse of power by governments of the day.
>
> (Gray 1995: 11)

Second, alongside the general attack on public life and specifically on the professions, there has been an erosion of local and community life. Powerful groups have disinvested in local communities and the effects on social fabric and life are clearly visible.

Third, in the newspapers, television and more generally, the quality of public knowledge has been in substantial decline over the past two decades. As in the USA, there has been a process of 'dumbing down' at work. The recent furore over the paparazzi is merely a symptom of the tabloidisation of public knowledge – balanced commentary declines and sensational stories increase.

In each of these cases, however, there is evidence of 'New Right overreach'. Let us take them in order, for they represent some of our opportunities to rejuvenate our public intellectual work.

First, the attack on the professionals: specifically here, the attack on the teaching profession. In terms of strategic politics, the alliance between teachers and externally located researchers is potentially very powerful. This is because the teacher unions, certainly their leaders, now realise that the attack on educational research and theory was an attack on teachers' professionalism. Professional groups traditionally trade on their underpinning theoretical bodies of knowledge. Without these they become technicians devoid of professional claims. Research and theory, and teacher unions pursuing profession and status, desperately need each other.

This provides an important coalition for reworking the relationship, and indeed the substance, of theory and practice. This time we must avoid the estrangements of foundational theory and develop engaged, practice-informing research and theory – especially new theories of educational inclusion.

Above all, we must see that only when practice and new forms of theory come together can educational research hope to have any hold on defining educational visions and on planning new educational structures. We must grasp the central historical point that theory and practice are not inevitably or intrinsically divorced: it is structures and institutionalised missions that have created the recent divorce. But new structures and institutionalised practices could consummate a new marriage. Historically, the relationship of theory to practice follows a cyclical pattern.

Certainly, histories of the relationship between theory and practice point to wide differentials in the gap between the two. Far from being wide and intractable, the dichotomy seems to be, at least partially, tractable and highly variable over time. Simon examined the relationship between theory and practice in three periods, 1880–1900, 1920–40 and 1940–60. In the first and last periods, he found a 'close relation between theory and practice'. For instance, in the period 1880–1900:

> For a whole concatenation of reasons, and from a variety of motives, it was thought that the masses should be educated, or at least schooled – and they were. This whole enterprise was, as it were, powered by an ideology – or theoretical stance – which emphasised the educability of the normal child, a view underpinned by advances in the field of psychology and physiology relating to human learning.
>
> (Simon 1985: 49)

The point underlined by the quote and the evidence about this historical period is that the potential for a close relationship, or, at the other extreme, no relationship, between theory and practice depends on the political conditions of the time, particularly as expressed in the social purposes and missions defined for our public schools.

So we have to return to the point of rupture in the 1970s, where increasingly divorced educational theory led to calls for applied research and a return to practice. This rupture was hijacked to develop a wholescale evacuation of theory and a return to classrooms and practice. From then on, the design of education was moved away from the intellectuals and the educationists, and firmly placed in the hands of politicians. Only new alliances between theory and practice can remake the possibility of educational research contributing to new visions and new structures of education.

The concern is how to develop collaborative modes in ways that maintain, revive and reinscribe theoretical and critical missions within teacher education. In current political times, this is clearly not an easy act to accomplish, even when thinking theoretically, but it does mean that we need to look closely at the potential collaboration between teachers and externally located researchers in faculties of education. Whilst I believe that the best mechanism for improving practice is for teachers, in an ongoing way, to research and reflect upon their practice, I do not believe that a narrow focus on practice in collaborating on research, a panacea that is politically popular at the moment, will take us very far. There are many reasons for this contention. Let me focus on two: first, education is far more than a practical matter. Practice constitutes a good deal more than the technical things teachers do in classrooms. Education is a personal matter as well as a political matter. The way teachers interact in classrooms relates in a considerable way to who they are and to their whole approach to life. It would be important, therefore, to have a collaborative form of research that links and analyses the teacher's life and work. Second, the interactive practices of classes are subject to constant change; particularly, at the moment, political and constitutional change. These often take the form of new government guidelines. To stay only with practice as a politically and socially constructed form is inevitably to involve teachers in the implementation and acceptance of initiatives that are generated elsewhere. This would make collaboration and research into a form of political quietism.

For these reasons, I would be against the notion that our focus for collaborative work between teachers and externally located researchers should be mainly upon practice. In some ways, regrettably, this is the logical outcome of the phrase 'teacher as researcher' (a movement whose value position I strongly support), for the converse is the 'researcher as teacher'. As we have noted, the teacher's work is politically and socially constructed. The parameters to practice, whether they are political or biographical, range over an extremely wide terrain. To narrow our focus to 'practice as defined' is to ensure that our collaborative work might fall victim to historical circumstance and political tendencies. At the moment, quite clearly, the New Right in many Western countries is seeking to transform teacher practice into the work of a technician, a trivialised and routine bureaucratic deliverer of pre-designed packages, guidelines and prejudices. To accept these definitions and to focus our collaboration and research on practice so defined is to play into their hands.

Whilst, of course, some of the more valuable critical and collaborative work has sought to critique and transcend the politically dominant definitions of practice, this does not avoid the substance of the critique. For by starting our research and collaboration, by focusing on practice in this way, the initiative for defining our very starting point has been conceded to politicians and bureaucrats. It is my profound belief that to sponsor more autonomous and critical collaborative work, we need to adopt a wider focus of enquiry. This lens of enquiry could take a number of forms. It could focus on critical incidents in teaching, as David Tripp has eloquently argued (Tripp 1994: 65–76). It could focus on theories of context, it could focus on the teacher's life and work or it could focus on the teacher's stories or narratives; it could also focus on public education more broadly conceived of than only schooling by concentrating on developing a 'learning society', as Young has argued (Goodson 1994). It should, in short, be possible to develop a broader approach for collaborative educational study in the future. Much of the emerging work in the areas I have listed now indicates that a rich flow of dialogue and data can be assembled through broadening our lens of enquiry and collaboration. Moreover, this broadened focus may (and I stress may) allow teachers greater authority and control in collaborative research than has often appeared to be the case with practice-oriented study. The focus in that work has been on teacher practice, almost on the teacher *as* practice. What is now required is a collaborative modality that listens above all to the person at whom 'development' and 'implementation' are aimed. This means that strategies should now be explored and developed which facilitate and maximise the potential for the teacher's voice to be heard in collaborative work. I believe that this strategy for developing collaboration and reinscribing the theoretical mission is well under way and it behoves us to push much harder to ensure that this kind of work sets up an articulate counterculture to the current initiatives that occupy 'the high ground' in so many Western countries.

This, then, is the response to New Right overreach on the professions. What of the vacuum left in community life and public knowledge? Here, there is an opportunity to define new strategies for curriculum and learning. If the National Curriculum concentrates on the uniform unifying of codes divorced from local communities, the opportunity is open to develop new links between education and community-building. What would a modern curriculum for community-building look like, as opposed to one looking back to a mythical golden age of nationhood? The appeal of such a vision of education would, I think, be substantial and would highlight many of the iniquitous structures currently in place.

Likewise, at the level of public knowledge, the deterioration in public information offers new opportunities for educational research and activity – looking at the full implications of developing a learning society and improving public education both inside and, at least as crucially, outside the school. Here, we should be researching and defining new patterns – for public education in a learning society. Curriculum should focus on the pupil as researcher and not only as the passive recipient of other people's knowledge.

At this stage of a new government, new visions and voices in educational research are needed to harness some of the forces that were active at the time of the elections. Without new visions we are stuck with the 'piecemeal pragmatism' that has affected our work for two decades. We have to find a new strategic politics and a way to create new pre-figurative sites.

Moreover, as the new government increases its call for a more professional teaching force, the alliance between research and theoretical knowledge and teaching will once again be forced on to the agenda. This time we have to be ready with a range of new collaborative perspectives and activities. These new perspectives need to stress educational research that acts as a kind of 'moral witness' to the initiatives that are undertaken. Hopefully, we can once again join in a world under construction and this time our intellectual inauguration needs to envision a 'new moral order' for schooling.

With this new moral order let me return you to Lawrence Stenhouse's last lecture. Here, he asked whether learning and critical literacy should be confined to an elite.

Our system (he said) is notable for being in the power of those who do not commit their own children to it and it is accordingly vulnerable. The powerful still do not favour the cultivation amongst the lower orders of the scepticism and critical intelligence that is valued amongst their betters. It is for that reason that they point backwards to basics in the face of the potential of the exciting curricula in literacy, numeracy and knowledge to be found in the recent curriculum movement, in the leading state schools and in the more enlightened private schools.

> At stake is more than 100 years of adventure beyond the mere basics, a span in which schools have – fitfully no doubt – tried to make people independent thinkers capable of participation in the democratic process and of deciding what the future of their society shall be like. Perhaps a faith in expansion and progress underlay that provision for the citizen. We must now find ways of ensuring that a defensive, and more apprehensive, establishment in the context of a contracting economy does not make a critical education an education reserved for privilege.
>
> (quoted in Simon 1990: 19–20)

In ending with Lawrence's quote, we see how our collective memory of a humane society continues to infuse our search for a new moral order for schooling and education. There could be no greater legacy for Lawrence Stenhouse's continuing relevance and his life's work.

References

Annan, N. (1995) *Our Age: The Generation that Made Post-war Britain*, London: Harper Collins.

Breines, W. (1980) 'Community and Organization', in 'The New Left and Michel's "Iron Law" ', *Social Problems*, 27(4), 419–29.

Burke, K. and Cairncross, A. (1992) *'Goodbye, Great Britain', The 1976 IMF Crisis* New Haven and London: Yale University Press.

CARE (1974) University of East Anglia, Norwich, 28 October, pp. 3–4, Chicago: University of Chicago Press.

Chomsky, N. (1995) 'A rebel with an endless cause', *The Times Higher Educational Supplement*, 23 June.

Clifford, G.J. and Guthrie, J.W. (1988) 'Ed School: A brief for professional education', *The Phi Delta Kappan*, 70(5), 380–85, published by Phi Delta Kappa International.

De Beauvoir, S. (1963) *Memoirs of a Dutiful Daughter*, Harmondsworth: Penguin.

Gauchet, M. (1994) 'Maman saps the soul of Sartre's city', *The Observer*, 18 September.

Giddy, D. (1807) 'The parliamentary debates – parochial schools bill, 2nd reading', p. 798, *Hansard*, London: Hansard, IX, 13 July.

Goodson, I.F. (1994) *Studying Curriculum: Cases and Methods*, New York: Teachers College Press and Buckingham: Open University Press.

Gray, J. (1995) 'Bite of the New Right', *The Guardian*, 23 October.

Halsey, A.H. (1992) *Decline of Donnish Dominion*, pp. 247–52, Oxford: Clarendon Press.

Kotarbinski, T. (1997) *Dictionary of Scientific Quotations*, by Alan MacKay, quoted in Kroto 'My cultural life', *The Guardian*, 2 April.

Lasch, C. (1995) *In Revolt of the Elites*, New York: Norton.

Macdonald, B. (1991) *Dictionary of Scientific Quotations*, by Alan MacKay, quoted in Rudduck 'My cultural life', *Guardian*, 2 April.

Marquand, D. (1994) 'There is such a thing as society', *The Guardian*, 16 July.

Mills, C.W. (1979) *Power, Politics and People*, New York: Oxford University Press.

Moore, S. (1994) 'Take it slowly from the end', *The Guardian*, 17 November.

Mulgan, G. and Worpole, K. (1994) 'Alien life in open space', *The Guardian*, 17 November.

Schools Council (1965) 'Raising the School Leaving Age', working paper 2, para. 60, in Rudduck, J. (1991) *Innovation and Change*, p. 9, London: Schools Council, Open University Press.

Shils, E. (1972) 'The Intellectual and the Powers (Chicago)', in Halsey, A.H. (1992) *Decline of Donnish Dominion*, p. 250, Oxford: Clarendon Press.

Simon, B. (1985) *Does Education Matter?* London: Lawrence & Wishart.

Simon, B. (1990) 'The National Curriculum, School Organisation and the Teacher', in Rudduck, J. (1995) *An Education that Empowers: A Collection of Lectures in Memory of Lawrence Stenhouse*, pp. 19–20, Clevedon: Multilingual Matters Ltd.

Stenhouse, L. (1974) 'CARE Discussion Paper', Mimeo: Norwich UEA.

Thompson, E.P. (1987) 'Diary', *London Review of Books*, 7 May.

Tripp, D. (1994) 'Teachers' lives, critical incidents, and professional practice', *International Journal of Qualitative Studies in Education*, 7, 65–76.

Williams, R. (1983) *The Times Higher Educational Supplement*, 'Intellectuals behind the scenes', 21 January.

10 Knowledge, personal narrative and the social future

In his recent analysis on education, Zygmun Bauman focused on the three types of learning identified by Mead (1964). Learning, in this analysis, divides into three linked but distinct types. There is the primary learning: 'first-degree learning' – the subterranean process of 'learning to learn'; 'first-degree learning of content learning' – the formal curriculum, so to speak. But there is also *deutero* – what we might call 'secondary learning' – the subterranean process of learning to learn.

Bauman says that this secondary learning:

> Depends not so much on the diligence and talents of the learners and the competence and assiduity of their teachers, as on the attributes of the world in which the former pupils are bound to live their lives.
>
> (Bauman 2001: 24)

'Tertiary learning' he summarises as learning: 'How to break the regularity, how to rearrange fragmentary experiences into heretofore unfamiliar patterns' (ibid.: 125).

'Tertiary learning' is about living without habits and routinised learning, it's about breaking away from pre-digested prescriptions of curriculum and moving to the definition, ownership and ongoing narration of our own curriculum.

Looking at these three types of learning should highlight the current crises of curriculum and of educational studies generally. The old patterns of curriculum development and curriculum study are utterly unsuited to the new society of risk, instability and rapid change in which we now live. They are locked into primary learning and prescription. Bauman says:

> I suggest that the overwhelming feeling of crises experienced by philosophers, theorists and practitioners of education alike, in a greater or a smaller measure, that current version of the 'living at the crossroads feeling', the feverish search for a new self-definition and ideally, a new identity as well – these have little to do with the faults, errors or negligence of the professional pedagogue or failures of educational theory, but quite a lot to do with the universal meeting of identities with the deregulation and privatization of

the identity – formation processes, the dispersal of authorities, the polyphony of the messages and ensuing fragmentation of life which characterizes the world we live in.

(Ibid.: 127)

Bauman, then, is clear that the crises of curriculum and of education are not an internal matter, a question of failures of practice or research – this is a broad question of positionality; people, and in this instance curriculum people, are searching for solutions in the wrong place.

Rather than writing new prescriptions for schools – new curriculum or new reform guidelines – they need to question the very validity of pre-digested prescriptions in a world of flux and change. We need, in short, to move from curriculum as prescription to curriculum as identity narration, from prescribed cognitive learning to life management narrative learning. It is this shift that I will try to outline in this chapter. First, I will deal with the definitive redundancy of curriculum as prescription, and second, I will tentatively outline the move to curriculum as narrative, which I believe marks the way to our new social future.

First, then, the established practice of curriculum as prescription on which so many assumptions of practitioners and researchers are based. The primacy of the ideology of 'curriculum as prescription' (CAP) can be evidenced in even a cursory glimpse at curriculum literature. This view of curriculum develops from a belief that we can dispassionately define the main ingredients of the course of study, and then proceed to teach the various segments and sequences in systematic turn. Despite the obvious simplicity, not to say crudity, of this view the 'objectives game' is still, if 'not the only game in town', certainly the main game. There may be many reasons for this continuing predominance, but explanatory potential is not, I think, one of the factors.

'Curriculum as prescription' supports important mystiques about state schooling and society. Most notably, CAP supports the mystique that expertise and control reside within central government, educational bureaucracies or the university community. Providing nobody exposes this mystique, the worlds of 'prescription rhetoric' and 'schooling as practice' can co-exist. Both sides benefit from such peaceful co-existence. The agencies of CAP are seen to be 'in control' and the schools are seen to be 'delivering' and can carve out a good degree of autonomy if they accept the rules. Curriculum prescriptions thereby set certain parameters, with transgression and occasional transcendence being permissible as long as the rhetoric of prescription and management is not challenged.

Of course there are 'costs of complicity' in accepting the myth of prescription: above all these involve, in various ways, an acceptance of established modes of power relations. Perhaps most importantly, the people intimately connected with the day-to-day social construction of curriculum and schooling, the teachers, are thereby effectively disenfranchised in the 'discourse of schooling'. To continue to exist, their day-to-day power must basically remain unspoken and unrecorded. This then is the price of complicity. The vestiges of day-to-day power and autonomy for schools and for teachers are dependent on continuing to accept the fundamental lie.

With regard to curriculum study the 'costs of complicity' are ultimately cata-strophic, for the historic compromise we have described has led to the displace-ment of a whole field of study. It has led to the directing of scholarship into fields that service the mystique of central and/or bureaucratic control. For scholars who benefit from maintaining this mystique – in the universities particularly – this complicity is, to say the least, self-serving.

Prescription and establishment of power make easy allies. As argued in my book, *The Making of Curriculum* (1995), curriculum was basically invented as a concept to direct and control the teacher's licence and potential freedom in the classroom. Over the years, the alliance between prescription and power has been carefully nurtured so that curriculum becomes a device to reproduce existing power relocation in society. The children of powerful, resourceful parents enjoy curriculum inclusion and the less advantaged suffer from curriculum exclusion. As Bordieu has argued, a parent's 'cultural capital' effectively buys success for their student offspring in this way.

To see how a prescribed curriculum works to exclude in a powerful and insid-ious way perhaps you will forgive a journey back to the historical past: an exam-ple from the experience of New Labour in Britain. This should have been a government showing some commitment to social inclusion and this commit-ment did exist in the rhetoric of government policy. In this sense it is perhaps a better guide to the complexities and contradictions of intentions which reflect a degree of social concern than the later episode of what we have called in Chapter 1 'corporate rule'.

After the election of a New Labour government in 1997, avowedly deter-mined to prioritise 'education, education, education', there has been a stated concern to broaden social inclusion. Given the well-established (and well-defended) patterns of social inequality in Britain, this was never going to be an easy task. It would seem that New Labour policies have in fact worked not to broaden social inclusion but to deepen social exclusion. Speaking on 26 July 2005 to the new Labour think-tank, the Institute of Public Policy Research, then Secretary of State for Education Ruth Kelly said:

> The gap between rich and poor in national curriculum test results and admissions to universities had grown. We must treat seriously the possibility that – despite all our efforts – who your parents are still affects attainment as much in 2004 as it did in 1998.
>
> (Game 2005: 17)

The key phrase in this statement is the phrase 'despite all our efforts'. Looking at the report again should raise our suspicions. Whilst she admits that 'who your parents are still affects attainment as much in 2004 as it did in 1998', her data actually show rather that New Labour policies have worked to increase, not to modify, the gap between rich and poor in educational attainment. Not so much a result 'despite all our efforts', but a result quite possibly 'because of all our efforts'. The data show that New Labour policies are not working towards social inclusion – they are actually furthering social exclusion.

Now a cynical reading of New Labour policies might argue that this government followed a policy of fine-tuning social exclusion by stealth. I do not take this view. Rather, I suspect we had a government with broadly good intentions that approached the task of social inclusion as a Christian and philanthropic duty. The educational background of the major players in government and their advisers and civil servants predisposed them to believe in social inclusion as a process of distributing elite educational categories more widely. They forgot that, as members of the elite, their educational experiences were founded on the social exclusions of others. What counted as education for them was designed for the few at the price of exclusion for the many.

As a result, they have quite possibly unknowingly employed educational strategies built around well-established foundations of exclusion to try to deliver social inclusion. This is not as illogical as an informed educational research reading might imply. Most of us equate 'education' with our own educational experiences and we accept as 'givens' basic educational phenomena such as 'traditional' school subjects or 'academic' examinations. These are part of the widely accepted 'grammar of schooling'. A layman's view would be that since 'these things equal good schooling', let's try and include more pupils in this kind of educational experience and we will thereby deliver social inclusion. This seems like common sense and certainly this was the way New Labour proceeded. In fact, the truth is far more complex and contradictory. We need to understand a little of the history of schooling to see why New Labour rushed so far and fast up an exclusionary cul-de-sac in pursuit of social inclusion.

To outline a section on the history of schooling I want to draw on the studies I have been undertaking for the last 30 years or so. They, too, have attempted to answer the question of why social inclusion and 'fair education for all' seems so perennially elusive. Broadly, what these studies show is that many of the traditional building blocks of schooling are themselves devices for social exclusion, not inclusion. Let me take as an example that unproblematic 'given' in every school – the 'traditional' school subject.

Exclusive pursuits: the invention of school subjects

To begin with, let me take an episode in the invention of one school subject: science. I choose this example to show the relationship between school subject knowledge, which is accepted and becomes therefore 'traditional', and subject knowledge, which is disallowed. This is the interface between school knowledge and powerful interest groups in society. School subjects are defined not in a disinterested scholastic way, but in close relationship to the power and interests of social groups. The more powerful the social group is, the more likely they are to exercise power over school knowledge.

In his book *Science for the People* (1973), David Layton describes a movement in the initial development of the school science curriculum called the 'Science of Common Things'. This was an early attempt to broaden social inclusion through relating the science curriculum to ordinary pupils' experience of the natural world, of their homes, daily lives and work. This curriculum was delivered in the elementary schools set up for predominantly working-class clienteles. There is clear evidence provided by Layton, and by contemporary government reports, that the Science of Common Things worked successfully in classrooms and extended science education. A successful strategy for social inclusion in school knowledge was therefore put in place.

We would, however, be wrong to assume that this was seen as a desirable development. Far from it: other definitions of school science were being advocated. Lord Wrottesley chaired a Parliamentary Committee of the British Association for the Advancement of Science on the most appropriate type of science education for the upper classes. Hodson argues that the Committee's report:

> reflected a growing awareness of a serious problem: that science education at the elementary level was proving highly successful, particularly as far as the development of thinking skills was concerned, and the social hierarchy was under threat because there was not corresponding development for the higher orders.
>
> (Goodson 1987: 36)

Lord Wrottesley's fears were clearly stated as regards moves to further social inclusion:

> a poor boy hobbled forth to give a reply; he was lame and humpbacked, and his wan, emaciated face told only too clearly the tale of poverty and its consequences ... but he gave forthwith so lucid and intelligent a reply to the question put to him that there arose a feeling of admiration for the child's talents combined with a sense of shame that more information should be found in some of the lowest of our lowest classes on matters of general interest than those far above them in the world by station.
>
> (Testimony of Lord Wrottesley before the Parliamentary Committee of the British Association for the Advancement of Sciences, 1860)

Wrottesley concluded: 'It would be an unwholesome and vicious state of society in which those who are comparatively unblessed with nature's gifts should be generally superior in intellectual attainments to those above them in station' (ibid.: 36–7).

Soon after Wrottesley's comments in 1860, science was removed from the elementary curriculum. When science eventually reappeared in the curriculum of elementary schools some 20 years later, it was in a very different form from the science of common things. A watered-down version of pure laboratory science had become accepted as the correct and 'traditional' view of science, a view which has persisted largely unchallenged to the present day. School subjects, it seems, have to develop a form acceptable to the 'higher orders' of society – being a mechanism for social inclusion naturally does not recommend itself to the higher orders, whose very position depends on social exclusion. School subjects thereafter become in themselves not only 'accepted', 'given', 'traditional' and inevitable, but also, in their academic form, exclusionary devices.

Fast-forwarding a century or more, I began to study a new subject – 'environmental studies'; not unlike the Science of Common Things in that it grew from its origins as a working-class inclusionary subject to begin to claim the status of 'a proper subject'. In my book *School Subjects and Curriculum Change* I show how this new subject, highly suited to comprehensive schools and with real inclusionary potential, was systematically blocked from becoming a broad-based, 'A' level 'academic' subject (Goodson 1993). In Britain, only a subject accepted as 'academic' can be resourced as a high-status, 'proper subject'.

This position of hierarchy for 'academic' subjects in fact represented a history of subjects linking to social hierarchy and social exclusion. The dominance of academic subjects goes back to the battle over which subjects should be prioritised in the new secondary schools at the start of the twentieth century. In 1904, Morant's Secondary Regulations handed victory to the public school-cum-grammar school vision of education and school subjects. Hence the academic subject was built on a clear foundation of social exclusion, for such ~~science~~ er catered for more than 20 per cent of pupils. In effect, the 'bottom' t were sacrificed and the top 20 per cent were promoted by the n of the 'academic tradition'. A contemporary noted of the Regulations that the academic subject-centred curriculum was 'subordinated to that literary instruction which makes for academic culture, but is of no practical utility to the classes for whom the local authorities should principally cater' (Eaglesham 1967: 59).

In the comprehensive schools, whilst new curriculum initiatives developed new subject categories such as environmental studies, but also community studies, urban studies, women's studies and social studies, the stranglehold of the academic tradition remained. This effectively blocked other traditions in subjects that stressed those vocational and pedagogic traditions likely to promote social inclusion. The very process of becoming a school subject therefore purges subject knowledge of its inclusionary characteristics. Layton shows this exclusionary effect with his evolutionary profile of the traditional subject. In the first stage:

> The callow intruder stakes a place in the timetable, justifying its presence on grounds such as pertinence and utility. During this stage learners are attracted to the subject because of its bearing on matters of concern to them. The teachers are rarely trained specialists, but bring the missionary enthusiasms of pioneers to their task. The dominant criterion is relevance to the needs and interests of the learners.
>
> (Layton 1972: 9)

In the interim second stage:

> A tradition of scholarly work in the subject is emerging along with a corps of trained specialists from which teachers may be recruited. Students are still attracted to the Study, but as much by its reputation and growing academic status as by its relevance to their own problems and concerns. The internal logic and discipline of the subject is becoming increasingly influential in the selection and organisation of subject matter.
>
> (Ibid.)

In the final stage:

> The teachers now constitute a professional body with established rules and values. The selection of subject matter is determined in large measure by the judgements and practices of the specialist scholars who lead inquiries in the field. Students are initiated into a tradition, their attitudes approaching passivity and resignation, a prelude to disenchantment.
>
> (Ibid.)

The central place of 'academic' subjects is ensconced in our secondary schools; so, therefore, is an inbuilt pattern of social prioritising and exclusion. The process outlined above shows clearly that school subject groups tend to move progressively away from social relevance or vocational emphasis. High status in the secondary school tends to focus on abstract theoretical knowledge divorced from the workaday world or the everyday world of the learner. To these high-status academic subjects go the main resources in our school systems: the better-qualified teachers, the favourable sixth form ratios and the pupils deemed most able. The link is now strengthened by New Labour initiatives in terms of targets, tests and league tables. In this way, a pattern of social prioritising built on exclusive pursuits found itself at the heart of a programme of social inclusion. Such a central contradiction and a range of other exclusionary devices, inherited unknowingly or unthinkingly, have contributed to the abject failure of New Labour policies to further social inclusion. It is urgently to be hoped that, the next time policies are formulated, relevant educational research in the area will at least be consulted and considered.

The underpinning prioritisation of academic school subjects effectively strangled new attempts to develop a more inclusive curriculum in comprehensive schools. This pattern of social prioritising was finally consolidated in the new National Curriculum of 1988, which almost exactly re-established Morant's Secondary Regulations of 1904 – the Public School and Grammar School Curriculum was firmly reinstated. A pattern of subject knowledge based on selective exclusion became the lynchpin of the curricula to be offered in comprehensive schools.

Into this stratified and exclusionary terrain came the New Labour government, preaching social inclusion and missionary morality. Their focus was on tightening up delivery of targets, tests and tables. But they never even questioned the exclusionary foundations on which their policies were to be built. In Britain were the leading researchers in the world on the history of school subjects and on the patterns described above. Not one of these researchers was ever consulted by government, whether New Labour or recent Tory. They pursued social inclusion employing a wide range of well-honed exclusionary devices. The results were precisely as Ruth Kelly recorded – the pronouncements in favour of social inclusion produced results that further extended social exclusion. Tony Blair, of Fettes College and Durham Cathedral School, and his offspring at the Oratory School, should have taken a moment to listen to an earlier Labour leader often pilloried because he stood firm on his principles and understood the complexity of the task of pursuing social inclusion in the face of elite opposition:

> We are not here in the world to find elegant solutions, pregnant with initiative, or to serve the ways and modes of profitable progress. No, we are here to provide for all those who are weaker and hungrier, more battered and crippled than ourselves. That is our only certain good and great purpose on earth, and if you ask me about those economic problems that may arise if the top is deprived of their initiatives I would answer 'to hell with them. The top is greedy and mean and will always find a way to take care of themselves. They always do.'
>
> (Foot 2001)

With the current Tory administration we now have a chance to test Foot's power of prophecy.

Curriculum as prescription and powerful interest groups are then locked in a potent historical partnership that structures curriculum in basic ways and effectively subverts any passing innovations or reforms. The prescriptions provide clear 'rules of the game' for schooling and finance, and resources are bred into these rules. Curriculum research, with a few honourable exceptions, has also tended to follow the 'rules of the game' by accepting curriculum as prescription as its starting point, even when in the odd case advocating resistance or transformation. The reason for hope now comes because, whilst the rules of the game for curriculum and for reproducing the social order are well established, the wider social order and associated rules of the game are now undergoing seismic change. This will destabilise the cosy alliance of power and prescription in unpredictable but definitive ways. The curriculum game is about to experience pulverising change, but often seems blissfully unaware of what the future holds.

In the new era of flexible work organisation, workers face unpredictable and constantly changing assignments:

> The types of skills required to practise flexible occupations do not on the whole demand long-term and systematic learning. More often than not, they transform a well-profiled logically coherent body of skills and habits from the asset it used to be, into the handicap it is now.
>
> (Bauman 2001: 132)

Long-established and prescribed courses of study therefore become a handicap to the new flexible work order. Curriculum as prescription might provide residual patterns of social reproduction, but its increasingly economic dysfunctionality calls, its continuity into question by powerful economic interests and global pressures. Bauman stated the dilemma with exquisite precision and with utter clarity for our curriculum futures:

> In our increasingly flexible and thoroughly deregulated job market all prospects of arresting the rot, let alone restoring the fast-vanishing framework of prospective planning, grow bleaker by the hour.
>
> (Ibid.: 131–2).

'Prospective planning' of learning – curriculum as prescription is then colossally inappropriate to the flexible work order – in this analysis is doomed and will require rapid replacement by new forms of learning organisation. Let us therefore look at some new notions of curriculum as narrative learning.

Curriculum as narration

In this section I want to give an example from research projects that I am currently involved with. The main project that addresses the issue of narrative learning is the Learning Lives project. Learning Lives is a four-year longitudinal study that aims to deepen our understanding of the meaning and significance of informal learning in the lives of adults and aims to identify ways in which adult learning can be supported and enhanced. It is funded, as part of the British government's Teaching and Learning Programme, by the Economic and Social Research Council. As well as informal learning, the project has begun to focus on what we call 'narrative learning'. 'Narrative learning' is the kind of learning that goes on in the elaboration and ongoing maintenance of a life narrative or identity. The kind of motifs that emerge in narrative learning are those such as the journey, the quest, the dream – all of them central motifs for the ongoing elaboration of a life mission. We have come to see this kind of narrative learning as central to the way in which people learn throughout their life course, and it requires a different form of research and elaboration to understand this kind of learning as opposed to the more traditional kinds of formal and informal learning. In investigating narrative learning, it is at this point that we begin to develop the concept of narrative capital.

To explain the meaning of narrative learning and narrative capital I want to provide an example of how this new mode of education works from different assumptions to those modes of learning that accept curriculum as prescription.

As we noted in an earlier section of this chapter, the established modalities of education and learning depend on curriculum as prescription and link closely to existing patterns of power and cultural capital. For Bordieu, cultural capital and indeed symbolic capital represent those aspects of dominant interest groups that can be commodified and credentialed as successful learning. In Britain, cultural capital is best evidenced in high-status public schools, which are in fact the schools where parents privately pay for their children to be educated. Schools such as Eton and Harrow would be classic examples of cultural capital, where the cultural domination of the group and the social networks that the schools afford access to provide enormous cultural capital for students learning in these institutions. In the traditional pattern of social reproduction, students with cultural capital effortlessly move into social elites and work with those that share similar patterns of cultural and social capital. Hence, curriculum as prescription, cultural and social capital and existing forms of social reproduction through schooling and education form a tripartite alliance of enduring power. But this power, as Bauman intimates in his own analysis, is now subject to considerable challenge in the new world of flexible work organisations. Here, the power of defining an organisational mission or life narrative becomes enormously important and can at certain times, even in this initial phase, undercut the old patterns of cultural capital and social elitism.

Nothing illustrates the shift from old hierarchies of cultural and symbolic capital towards something we might call 'narrative capital' better than the case of David Cameron, the leader of the Tory party in Britain (see Goodson 2005 and this volume p. 67).

In the Learning Lives project, we have the chance to see how life history can elucidate learning responses. What we do in the project is deal with learning as one of the strategies people employ as the response to events in their lives. The great virtue of this situation of our understanding of learning within the whole life context is that we get some sense of the issue of engagement in learning as it relates to people living their lives. When we see learning as a response to actual events, then the issue of engagement can be taken for granted. So much of the literature on learning fails to address this crucial question of 'engagement' and, as a result, learning is seen as some formal task that is unrelated to the needs and interests of the learner, hence so much of curriculum planning is based on prescriptive definitions of what is to be learnt without any understanding of the situation within the learners' lives. As a result, a vast amount of curriculum planning is abortive because the learner simply does not engage; hence to see learning as located within a life history is to understand that learning is contextually situated and that it also has a history, both in terms of the individual's life story and the history and trajectories of the institutions that offer formal learning opportunities, as well as the histories of the communities and locations in which informal learning takes place. In terms of transitional spaces, we can see learning as a response to incidental transitions, such as events related to illness, unemployment and domestic dysfunction, as well as the more structured transitions related to credentialing or retirement.

The way that our 'life history interviewees' describe learning often eloquently states the shift from traditional patterns of curriculum as prescription and learning by content into a more elaborated notion of narrative learning. The following quote, which I give at length, provides us with a clear evaluation of the different forms of learning given by one of our life history subjects:

Well I suppose the first thing that comes is, is the different kinds of, of learning that's, that I've done in, in my life from acquiring skills or acquiring languages – which, which entails something that you, you had absolutely no idea before and when you learn you *can* actually *do* it and you didn't know that you would be able to in the beginning and it really gives you a sense of empowerment. That's, I think that's, I mean, that's lifelong, a lifelong process because I'm still, I'm still learning how to play the violin, and I will be until, until the end and I'm still acquiring hopefully new languages, so that's, that's two things that, that I know that I'll continue, hopefully progressing in. And then there's, there's learning about, about how to be a social person in a, in a given environment, which entails in my case because I have to kind of translate myself from country to country, learning how the rules function in any given, given space, or given space that you live in, and they change, it's like goalposts that change, keep changing, so you have to translate your behaviour in certain ways. And you learn that something that you, something that's fine in one society, how you perceive completely differently. That is definitely a process of, of learning, and it's a two-fold thing because you learn about the society that you are in but you also learn about yourself and how you react to it. And then I guess the third thing is, would be, learning about yourself as a person and how you deal with, with life as, you know, in general, and that's also a lifelong, lifelong process, of how to, how to become what you think a person should be, a good person or a bad person or whatever person, whatever sort of person, and you work, you work on that. Try to examine your, your own behaviour and your relationship with, with the world and try to make sense of why things happen to you, why your reaction has brought up a certain, certain thing, and how the circumstances affected you in reacting a certain way, so it's a self-examination I suppose, but that's maybe the third kind of level of, of learning. I think, I think that's it. I think that's basically the three, the three things that I can think of off the top of my head.

(Learning Lives interview, 2 November 2008)

The narrative learning defined by our life story subject 'learning to be a social person in a given environment' and learning about yourself as a person and defining an identity project comes close to the notion of tertiary learning defined by Bateson. The curriculum shift we are seeing is from primary learning and curriculum as prescription to tertiary learning and curriculum as narration. This shift will accelerate rapidly as the move to flexible economic organisation takes place. The contextual inertia of a content-based curriculum of prescription will not endure in the fast-changing global world order. Bauman puts it this way:

Preparing for life – that perennial, invariable task of all education – must mean first and foremost cultivation of the ability to live daily and at peace with uncertainty and ambivalence, with a variety of standpoints and the absence of unerring and trustworthy authority.

(Bauman 2001: 138)

No better warning against the supreme inadequacies of the authoritative pre-scription of curriculum could be given: the qualities that are needed are 'fortify-ing critical and self-critical faculties', developing people's capacities to define and narrate their life purposes and missions in a fast-changing environment. Bauman notes:

> The point is ... that such qualities can hardly be developed in full through that aspect of the educational process which lends itself best to the design-ing and controlling powers of the theorists and practitioners of education through the verbally explicit contents of curriculum.
>
> (Ibid.)

Curriculum as prescription and primary learning of predetermined content, he is telling us, is a game that is coming to an end. He says: 'Educational philosophy and theory face the unfamiliar task of theorising a formative process which is not guided from the start by the target form designed in advance' (ibid.: 139).

If curriculum as prescription is ending, the new era of curriculum in the new social future is, we have to admit, far from clear in the sketches provided here of narrative learning and narrative capital, which, I believe, is the genesis of a new specification for curriculum. We are only at the beginning. It is a beginning that provides hope that we can finally heal the 'fundamental lie' that sits at the heart of curriculum as prescription. In the new social future, we must hope that cur-riculum will engage with the life missions, passions and purposes that people articulate in their lives. Now that would truly be a curriculum for empower-ment. Moving from authoritative prescription and primary learning to narrative empowerment and tertiary learning would transform our educational institu-tions and make them live out their early promise to help in changing their stu-dents' social future.

References

Bauman, Z. (2001) *The Individualized Society*, Cambridge: Polity Cambridge Press.
Bentham, M. (2005) 'Am I too posh to push?', *The Observer*, 15 May.
Eaglesham, E.J.R. (1967) *The Foundations of Twentieth-Century Education in England*, London: Routledge and Kegan Paul, pp. 59.
Foot, M. (2001) 'Best Foot goes ever forward', *The Observer*, 4 March.
Game, R. (2005) 'Educational reforms and the better off', *The Independent*, 2 June.
Goodson, I.F. (1987) (ed.) *International Perspectives in Curriculum History*, London: Croon Helm.
Goodson, I.F. (1993) *School Subjects and Curriculum Change*, 3rd edition, London and New York: Falmer Press.
Goodson, I.F. (1995) *The Making of Curriculum*, London and New York: Falmer Press.
Goodson, I.F. (2005) *Learning Curriculum and Life Politics*, London and New York: Routledge.
Layton, D. (1972) 'Science as general education', *Trends in Education*, 25, 12.
Layton, D. (1973) *Science for the People*, London: George Allen and Unwin.

Learning Lives (2003–7) 'Learning lives: learning, identity and agency in the life course', ESRC Teaching and Learning Research programme, with G. Biesta and F. Macleod, University of Exeter; J. Field, University of Stirling; and P. Hodkinson, University of Leeds. Available at: www.tlrp.org/proj/phase111/biesta.htm (accessed on 15 November 2013).

Mead, M. (1964) *Continuity in Cultural Evolution*, New Haven: Yale University Press.

Index